POETRY

AND

THE AGE

Randall Jarrell

POETRY

AND

THE AGE

The Noonday Press

A DIVISION OF

Farrar, Straus and Giroux

NEW YORK

Acknowledgment is hereby made for permission to quote from the following: LOUGH
DERG, *copyright 1946 by Denis Devlin, used by permission of Harcourt, Brace &*
Co. LORD WEARY'S CASTLE, *copyright 1944, 1946 by Robert Lowell, used by per-*
mission of Harcourt, Brace & Co. THE MILLS OF THE KAVANAUGHS, *copyright 1946,*
1947, 1948, 1950, 1951, by Robert Lowell, used by permission of Harcourt, Brace &
Co. CEREMONY AND OTHER POEMS, *copyright 1948, 1949, 1950 by Richard Wilbur,*
used by permission of Harcourt, Brace & Co. SELECTED POEMS, *copyright 1938 by*
New Directions, used by permission of the publisher. PATERSON, *copyright 1946,*
1948 by William Carlos Williams, used by permission of New Directions. THE
GREEN WAVE, *copyright by Muriel Rukeyser, used by permission of the author.* COL-
LECTED POEMS, *copyright 1951 by Marianne Moore, used by permission of The*
Macmillan Company. COMPLETE POEMS OF ROBERT FROST, *copyright 1930, 1947,*
1949 by Henry Holt & Co., Inc. Copyright 1936, 1942 by Robert Frost. Used by per-
mission of the publisher. THE COLLECTED POEMS OF A. E. HOUSMAN, *copyright 1936*
by Barclays Bank Ltd. Copyright 1940 by Henry Holt & Co., Inc. Used by permis-
sion of the publisher. NORTH AND SOUTH, *copyright 1946 by Elizabeth Bishop, used*
by permission of Houghton Mifflin Co. SELECTED POEMS *by John Crowe Ransom,*
copyright 1924, 1927, 1939, 1945 by Alfred A. Knopf, Inc., used by permission of
the publisher. HARMONIUM *by Wallace Stevens, copyright 1923, 1931 by Alfred A.*
Knopf, Inc., used by permission of the publisher. THE AURORAS OF AUTUMN, *copy-*
right 1947, 1948, 1949, 1950 by Wallace Stevens, used by permission of Alfred A.
Knopf, Inc.

TO

Mary von Schrader

Preface

THESE ARE CRITICISMS of a good many of the best, some of
the better, and a few of the worse American poets. Besides this,
there are criticisms of several English and French poets, and two
general essays on poetry and criticism in our time. Several of the
American poets I like most—Eliot and Dickinson, for instance—
I've never written about; I mean to write about them later. I
have written so much about Auden's poetry that the articles
and lectures make two-thirds of a book; consequently, they
aren't included here.

All these pieces—with the exception of the introduction to
William Carlos Williams' *Selected Poems*—have been published
in magazines, some of them in different shape. I want to thank
Partisan Review, *The Nation*, *The Kenyon Review*, *The New
York Times Book Review*, and *Perspectives U. S. A.* both for
printing them and for allowing me to reprint them. *The Obscurity of the Poet* was given as a lecture at Harvard University,
during a "conference" called The Defense of Poetry.

Preface

Contents

CONTENTS

POETRY

AND

THE AGE

The Obscurity of the Poet

WHEN I was asked to talk about the Obscurity of the Modern Poet I was delighted, for I have suffered from this obscurity all my life. But then I realized that I was being asked to talk not about the fact that people don't read poetry, but about the fact that most of them wouldn't understand it if they did: about the difficulty, not the neglect, of contemporary poetry. And yet it is not just modern poetry, but poetry, that is today obscure. *Paradise Lost* is what it was; but the ordinary reader no longer makes the mistake of trying to read it—instead he glances at it, weighs it in his hand, shudders, and suddenly, his eyes shining, puts it on his list of the ten dullest books he has ever read, along with *Moby Dick*, *War and Peace*, *Faust*, and Boswell's *Life of Johnson*. But I am doing this ordinary reader an injustice: it was not the Public, nodding over its lunch-pail, but the educated reader, the reader the universities have trained, who a few weeks ago, to the Public's sympathetic delight, put together this list of the world's dullest books.

Since most people know about the modern poet only that he is *obscure*—*i.e.*, that he is *difficult*, *i.e.*, that he is *neglected*—they naturally make a causal connection between the two meanings of the word, and decide that he is unread because he is difficult. Some of the time this is true; some of the time the reverse is true: the poet seems difficult *because* he is not read, *because* the reader is not accustomed to reading his or any other poetry. But most of the time neither is a cause—both are no more than effects of that long-continued, world-overturning cultural and social revolution (seen at its most advanced stage here in the United States) which has made the poet difficult and the public unused to any poetry exactly as it has made poet and public divorce their wives, stay away from church, dislike bull-baiting, free the slaves, get insulin shots for diabetes, or do a hundred thousand other things, some bad, some good, and some indifferent. It is superficial to extract two parts from this world-high whole, and to say of them: "This one, here, is the cause of that one, there; and that's all there is to it."

If we were in the habit of reading poets their obscurity would not matter; and, once we are out of the habit, their clarity does not help. Matthew Arnold said, with plaintive respect, that there was hardly a sentence in *Lear* that he hadn't needed to read two or three times; and three other appreciable Victorian minds, Beetle, Stalky, and McTurk, were even harder on it. They are in their study; Stalky reads:

Never any.
It pleased the king his master, very late,
To strike at me, upon his misconstruction,

When he, conjunct, and flattering in his displeasure,
Tripped me behind: being down, insulted, railed,
And put upon him such a deal of man
That worthy'd him, got praises of the King
For him attempting who was self-subdued;
And, in the fleshment of this dread exploit,
Drew me on here.

Stalky says: "Now, then, my impassioned bard, *construez!* That's Shakespeare"; and Beetle answers, "at the end of a blank half minute": "Give it up! He's drunk." If schoolboys were forced to read "The Phoenix and the Turtle," what *would* Beetle have said of these two stanzas?

Property was thus appalled
That the self was not the same;
Single nature's double name
Neither two nor one was called,

Reason, in itself confounded,
Saw division grow together;
To themselves yet either-neither,
Simple were so well compounded. . . .

You and I can afford to look at Stalky and Company, at Arnold, with dignified superiority: we know what those passages mean; we know that Shakespeare is never *obscure,* as if he were some modernist poet gleefully pasting puzzles together in his garret. Yet when we look at a variorum Shakespeare—with its line or two of text at the top of the page, its forty or fifty lines of wild surmise and quarrelsome conjecture at the bottom—we are troubled. When the Alexandrian poet Lycophron refers—and he is rarely so simple—to the *centipede, fair-faced, stork-hued daughters of Phalacra*, and they turn out to be boats, one ascribes this to Alexandrian decadence; but then one remembers that Welsh and Irish and Norse poets, the poets of a hundred barbarous cultures, loved nothing so much as referring to the very dishes on the table by elaborate descriptive epithets—periphrases, kennings—which their hearers had to be specially educated to understand. (Loved nothing so much, that is, except riddles.) And just consider the amount of classical allusions that those polite readers, our ancestors, were expected to recognize—and did recognize. If I recite to you, *The brotherless Heliades/ Melt in such amber tears as these*, many of you will think, *Beautiful;* a good many will think, *Marvell;* but how many of you will know to whom Marvell is referring?

Yet the people of the past were not repelled by this obscurity (seemed, often, foolishly to treasure it); nor are those peoples of the present who are not so far removed from the past as we: who have preserved, along with the castles, the injustice, and the social discrimination of the past, a remnant of its passion for reading poetry. It is hard to be much more difficult than Mallarmé; yet when I went from bookstore to bookstore in Paris, hunting for one copy of Corbière, I began to feel a sort of mocking frustration at the poems by Mallarmé, letters by Mallarmé, letters to Mallarmé, biographies of, essays on, and homage to Mallarmé with which the shelves of those bookstores tantalized me. For how long now the French poet has been writing as if the French public did not exist—as if it were, at best, a swineherd dreaming of that faraway princess the poet; yet it looks at him with traditional awe, and reads in dozens of literary newspapers, scores of literary magazines, the details of his life, opinions, temperament, and appearance. And in the Germanic countries people still glance at one with attentive respect, as if they thought that one might at any moment be about to write a poem; I shall never forget hearing a German say, in an objective considering tone, as if I were an illustration in a book called *Silver Poets of the Americas:* "You know, he looks a little like Rilke." In several South American countries poetry has kept most of the popularity and respect it formerly enjoyed; in one country, I believe Venezuela, the president, the ambassador whom he is sending to Paris, and the waiter who serves their coffee will four out of five times be poets. "What sort of poetry do *these* poets write?" is a question of frightening moment for us poor Northern poets; if the answer is, "Nice simple stuff," we shall need to question half our ways. But these poets, these truly popular poets, seem to have taken as models for their verse neither the poems of Homer, of Shakespeare, nor of Racine, but those of Pablo Picasso: they are all surrealists.

Is Clarity the handmaiden of Popularity, as everybody automatically assumes? how much does it help to be immediately plain? In England today few poets are as popular as Dylan Thomas—his magical poems have corrupted a whole generation of English poets; yet he is surely one of the most obscure poets who ever lived. Or to take an opposite example: the poems of the students of Yvor Winters are quite as easy to understand as those which Longfellow used to read during the Children's Hour; yet they are about as popular as those other poems (of their own composition) which *grave Alice, and laughing Allegra, and*

Edith with golden hair used to read to Longfellow during the Poet's Hour. If Dylan Thomas is obscurely famous, such poets as these are clearly unknown.

When someone says to me something I am not accustomed to hearing, or do not wish to hear, I say to him: *I do not understand you;* and we respond in just this way to poets. When critics first read Wordsworth's poetry they felt that it was silly, but many of them *said*, with Byron, that "he who understands it would be able/ To add a story to the Tower of Babel." A few years before, a great critic praising the work of that plainest of poets, John Dryden, had remarked that he "delighted to tread on the brink where sense and nonsense mingle." Dryden himself had found Shakespeare's phrases "scarcely intelligible; and of those which we understand some are ungrammatical, others coarse; and his whole style is so pestered with figurative expressions that it is as affected as it is coarse." The reviewers of "The Love Song of J. Alfred Prufrock," even those who admired it most, found it almost impossible to understand; that it was hopelessly obscure seemed to them self-evident. Today, when college girls find it exactly as easy, exactly as hard, as "The Bishop Orders his Tomb at St. Praxed's," one is able to understand these critics' despairing or denunciatory misunderstanding only by remembering that the first generation of critics spoke of Browning's poem in just the terms that were later applied to Eliot's. How long it takes the world to catch up! Yet it really never "catches up," but is simply replaced by another world that does not need to catch up; so that when the old say to us, "What shall I do to understand Auden (or Dylan Thomas, or whoever the latest poet is)?" we can only reply: "You must be born again." An old gentleman at a party, talking to me about a poem we both admired, the *Rubaiyat*, was delighted to find that our tastes agreed so well, and asked me what modern poet I like best. Rather cutting my coat to his cloth, I answered: "Robert Frost." He looked at me with surprise, and said with gentle but undisguised finality: "I'm afraid he is a little after my time." This happened in 1950; yet surely in 1850 some old gentleman, fond of Gray and Cowper and Crabbe, must have uttered to the young Matthew Arnold the same words, but this time with reference to the poetry of William Wordsworth.

We cannot even be sure what people will find obscure; when I taught at Salzburg I found that my European students did not find "The Waste Land" half as hard as Frost's poetry, since one went with, and the other against, all their own cultural presuppositions; I had not simply to explain "Home-Burial" to them, I had to persuade them that it was a poem. And another example occurs to me: that of Robert Hillyer. In a review of *The Death of Captain Nemo* that I read, the reviewer's first complaint was that the poem is obscure. I felt as if I had seen Senator McCarthy denounced as an agent of the Kremlin; for how could Mr. Hillyer be obscure?

That the poet, the modern poet, is, understandably enough, for all sorts of good reasons, more obscure than even he has any imaginable right to be—this is one of those great elementary (or, as people say nowadays, *elemental*) attitudes about which it is hard to write anything that is not sensible and gloomily commonplace; one might as well talk on faith and works, on heredity and environment, or on that old question: why give the poor bath-tubs when they only use them to put coal in? Anyone knows enough to reply to this question: "They don't; and, even if they did, *that's* not the reason you don't want to help pay for the tubs." Similarly, when someone says, "I don't read modern poetry because it's all stuff that nobody on earth can understand," I know enough to be able to answer, though not aloud: "It isn't; and, even if it were, *that's* not the reason you don't read it." Any American poet under a certain age, a fairly advanced age—the age, one is tempted to say, of Bernard Shaw— has inherited a situation in which no one looks at him and in which, consequently, everyone complains that he is invisible: for that corner into which no one looks is always dark. And people who have inherited the custom of not reading poets justify it by referring to the obscurity of the poems they have never read—since most people decide that poets are obscure very much as legislators decide that books are pornographic: by glancing at a few fragments someone has strung together to disgust them. When a person says accusingly that he can't understand Eliot, his tone implies that most of his happiest hours are spent at the fireside among worn copies of the *Agamemnon*, *Phèdre*, and the Symbolic Books of William Blake; and it is melancholy to find, as one commonly will, that for months at a time he can be found pushing eagerly through the pages of *Gone with the Wind* or *Forever Amber*, where *with head, hands, wings, or feet* this poor fiend *pursues his way, and swims, or sinks, or wades, or creeps, or flies;* that all his happiest memories of Shakespeare seem to come from a high school production of *As You Like It* in which he played the wrestler Charles; and that he has, by some obscure process of free association, com bined James Russell, Amy, and Robert Lowell into one majestic whole: a bearded cigar-smoking ambassador to the Vatican who, after accompanying Theodore Roosevelt on his first African expedition, came home to dictate on his deathbed the "Concord Hymn." Many a man, because Ezra Pound is too obscure for him, has shut forever the pages of *Paradise Lost;* or so one would gather, from the theory and practice such people combine.

The general public [in this lecture I hardly speak of the happy few, who grow fewer and unhappier day by day] has set up a criterion of its own, one by which every form of contemporary art is condemned. This criterion is, in the case of music, melody; in the case of painting, representation; in the case of poetry, clarity. In each case one simple aspect is made the test of a complicated whole, becomes a sort of loyalty oath for the work of art. Although judging by this method is almost as irrelevant as having the artist pronounce *shibboleth*, or swear that he is not a Know-Nothing, a Locofocoist, or a Bull Moose, it is as attractive, in exactly the same way, to the public that judges: instead of having to perceive, to enter, and to interpret those new worlds which new works of art are, the public can notice at a glance whether or not these pay lip-service to its own "principles," and can then praise or blame them accordingly. Most of the music of earlier centuries, of other continents, has nothing the public can consider a satisfactory melody; the tourist looking through the galleries of Europe very soon discovers that most of the Old Masters were not, representationally speaking, half so good as the painters who illustrate *Collier's Magazine;* how difficult and dull the inexperienced reader would find most of the great poetry of the past, if he could ever be induced to read it! Yet it is always in the name of the easy past that he condemns the difficult present.

Anyone who has spent much time finding out what people do when they read a poem, what poems actually mean for them, will have discovered that a surprising part of the difficulty they have comes from their almost systematic unreceptiveness, their queer unwillingness to pay attention even to the reference of pronouns, the meaning of the punctuation, which subject goes with which verb, and so on; "after all," they seem to feel, "I'm not reading *prose*." You need to read good poetry with an attitude that is a mixture of sharp intelligence and of willing emotional empathy, at once penetrating and generous: as if you were listening to *The Marriage of Figaro*, not as if you were listening to *Tristan* or to Samuel Butler's Handelian oratorios; to read poetry—as so many readers do—like Mortimer Snerd pretending to be Dr. Johnson, or like Uncle Tom recollecting Eva, is hardly to read poetry at all. When you begin to read a poem you are entering a foreign country whose laws and language and life are a kind of translation of your own; but to accept it because its stews taste exactly like your old mother's hash, or to reject it because the owl-headed goddess of wisdom in its temple is fatter than the Statue of Liberty, is an equal mark of that want of imagination, that inaccessibility to experience, of which each of us who dies a natural death will die.

That the poetry of the first half of this century often *was* too difficult—just as the poetry of the eighteenth century *was* full of antitheses, that of the metaphysicals full of conceits, that of the Elizabethan dramatists full of rant and quibbles—is a truism that it would be absurd to deny. How our poetry got this way—how romanticism was purified and exaggerated and "corrected" into modernism; how poets carried all possible tendencies to their limits, with more than scientific zeal; how the dramatic monologue, which once had depended for its effect upon being a departure from the norm of poetry, now became in one form or another the norm; how poet and public stared at each other with righteous indignation, till the poet said, "Since you won't read me, I'll make sure you can't"—is one of the most complicated and interesting of stories. But Modernism was not "that lion's den from which no tracks return," but only a sort of canvas whale from which Jonah after Jonah, throughout the late '20's and early '30's, made a penitent return, back to rhyme and metre and plain broad Statement; how many young poets to-day are, if nothing else, plain! Yet how little posterity—if I may speak of that imaginary point where the poet and the public intersect—will care about all the tendencies of our age, all those good or bad intentions with which ordinary books are paved; and how much it will care for those few poems which, regardless of intention, manage at once to sum up, to repudiate, and to transcend both the age they appear in and the minds they are produced by. One judges an age, just as one judges a poet, by its best poems—after all, most of the others have disappeared; when posterity hears that our poems are obscure, it will smile indifferently—just as we do when we are told that the Victorians were sentimental, the Romantics extravagant, the Augustans conventional, the metaphysicals conceited, and the Elizabethans bombastic—and go back to its (and our) reading: to Hardy's "During Wind and Rain," to Wordsworth's story of the woman

Margaret, to Pope's "Epistle to Dr. Arbuthnot," to Marvell's "Horatian Ode," to Shakespeare's *Antony and Cleopatra*, to Eliot's *Four Quartets*, and to all the rest of those ageless products of an age.

In this age, certainly, poetry persists under many disadvantages. Just as it has been cut off from most of the people who in another age would have read it, so it has been cut off from most of the people who in another age would have written it. Today poems, good poems, are written almost exclusively by "born poets." We have lost for good the poems that would have been written by the modern equivalents of Henry VIII or Bishop King or Samuel Johnson; born novelists, born theologians, born princes; minds with less of an innate interest in words and more of one in the world which produces words. We are accustomed to think of the poet, when we think of him at all, as someone Apart; yet was there—as so many poets and readers of poetry seem to think—*was* there in the Garden of Eden, along with Adam and Eve and the animals, a Poet, the ultimate ancestor of Robert P. Tristram Coffin? . . . When I last read poems in New York City, a lady who, except for bangs, a magenta jersey blouse, and the expression of Palamède de Charlus, was indistinguishable from any other New Yorker, exclaimed to me about a poet whom the years have fattened for the slaughter: "He read like a young god." I felt that the next poet was going to be told that I read like the young Joaquin Miller; for this lady was less interested in those wonderful things poems than in those other things, poets—not realizing that it is their subordination to the poems they write that makes them admirable. She seemed to me someone who, because he has inherited a pearl necklace, can never again look at an oyster without a shudder of awe. And this reminds one that, today, many of the readers a poet would value most have hardly learned to read any poetry; and many of those who regularly read his poems have values so different from his that he is troubled by their praise, and vexed but reassured by their blame.

Tomorrow morning some poet may, like Byron, wake up to find himself famous—for having written a novel, for having killed his wife; it will not be for having written a poem. That is still logically, but no longer socially, possible. Let me illustrate with a story. I once met on a boat, travelling to Europe with his wife and daughter, a man with whom I played ping-pong. Having learned from a friend that I wrote poetry, he asked one day with uninterested politeness, "Who are the American poets you like best?" I said, "Oh, T. S. Eliot, Robert Frost." Then this man—this father who every night danced with his daughter with the well-taught, dated, decorous attractiveness of the hero of an old *Saturday Evening Post* serial by E. Phillips Oppenheim; who had had the best professional in Los Angeles teach his wife and daughter the tennis strokes he himself talked of with wearying authority; who never in his life had gone through a doorway before anyone over the age of seven—this well-dressed, well-mannered, travelled, urbane, educated gentleman said placidly: "I don't believe I've heard of them." For so far as literature, the arts, philosophy, and science were concerned, he might better have been the policeman on the corner. But he was perfectly correct in thinking—not that he had ever thought about it—that a knowledge of these things is not an essential requirement of the society of which he is a part. We belong to a culture whose old hierarchy of values—which demanded that a girl read Pope just as it demanded that she go to church and play the pianoforte—has virtually disappeared; a culture in which the great artist or scientist, in the relatively infrequent cases in which he has become widely known, has the status of Betty Grable or of the columnist who writes that, the night before, he met both these "celebrities" at the Stork Club.

When, a hundred and fifty years ago, a man had made his fortune, he found it necessary to provide himself with lace, carriages, servants, a wife of good family, a ballerina, a fencing master, a dancing master, a chaplain, a teacher of French, a string quartet perhaps, the editions of Pope and Steele and Addison through which he worked a laborious way on unoccupied evenings: there was so much for him to learn to *do*, there in his new station in life, that he must often have thought with nostalgia of the days in which all that he had to do was make his fortune. We have changed most of that: in our day the rich are expected not to do but to be; and those ties, tenuous, ambiguous, and immemorial, which bound to the Power of a state its Wisdom and its Grace, have at last been severed.

When Mill and Marx looked at a handful of workingmen making their slow firm way through the pages of Shelley or Herbert Spencer or *The Origin of Species*, they thought with confident longing, just as Jefferson and Lincoln had, of the days when every man would be literate, when an actual democracy would make its choices with as much wisdom as any imaginary state where the philosopher is king; and no gleam of prophetic insight came to show them those workingmen, two million strong, making their easy and pleasant way through the pages of the

16

New York *Daily News*. The very speeches in which Jefferson and Lincoln spoke of their hope for the future are incomprehensible to most of the voters of that future, since the vocabulary and syntax of the speeches are more difficult—more obscure —than anything the voters have read or heard. For when you defeat me in an election simply because you were, as I was not, born and bred in a log cabin, it is only a question of time until you are beaten by someone whom the pigs brought up out in the yard. The truth that all men are politically equal, the recognition of the injustice of fictitious differences, becomes a belief in the fictitiousness of differences, a conviction that it is reaction or snobbishness or Fascism to believe that any individual differences of real importance can exist. We dislike having to believe in what Goethe called inborn or innate merits; yet—as a later writer more or less says—many waiters are born with the taste of duchesses, and most duchesses are born (and die) with the tastes of waiters: we can escape from the level of society, but not from the level of intelligence, to which we were born.

One of our universities recently made a survey of the reading habits of the American public; it decided that forty-eight percent of all Americans read, during a year, no book at all. I picture to myself that reader—non-reader, rather; one man out of every two—and I reflect, with shame: "Our poems are too hard for him." But so, too, are *Treasure Island, Peter Rabbit*, pornographic novels—any book whatsoever. The authors of the world have been engaged in a sort of conspiracy to drive this American away from books; have, in 77 million out of 160 million cases, succeeded. A sort of dream-situation often occurs to me in which I call to this imaginary figure, "Why don't you read books?"—

and he always answers, after looking at me steadily for a long time: "Huh?"

If my tone is mocking, the tone of someone accustomed to helplessness, this is natural: the poet is a condemned man for whom the State will not even buy breakfast—and as someone said, "If you're going to hang me, you mustn't expect to be able to intimidate me into sparing your feelings during the execution." The poet lives in a world whose newspapers and magazines and books and motion pictures and radio stations and television stations have destroyed, in a great many people, even the capacity for understanding real poetry, real art of any kind. The man who monthly reads, with vacant relish, the carefully predigested sentences which the *Reader's Digest* feeds to him as a mother pigeon feeds her squabs—this man *cannot* read the *Divine Comedy*, even if it should ever occur to him to try: it is too obscure. Yet one sort of clearness shows a complete contempt for the reader, just as one sort of obscurity shows a complete respect. Which patronizes and degrades the reader, the *Divine Comedy* with its four levels of meaning, or the *Reader's Digest* with its one level so low that it seems not a level but an abyss into which the reader consents to sink? The writer's real dishonesty is to give an easy paraphrase of the hard truth. Yet the average article in our magazines gives any subject whatsoever the same coat of easy, automatic, "human" interest; every year *Harper's Magazine* sounds more like *Life* and the *Saturday Evening Post*. Goethe said, "The author whom a lexicon can keep up with is worth nothing"; Somerset Maugham says that the finest compliment he ever received was a letter in which one of his readers said: "I read your novel without having to look up a single word in the dictionary." These writers, plainly, lived in different worlds.

Since the animal organism thinks, truly reasons, only when it is required to, thoughtfulness is gradually disappearing among readers; and popular writing has left nothing to the imagination for so long now that imagination too has begun to atrophy. Almost all the works of the past are beginning to seem to the ordinary reader flat and dull, because they do not supply the reader's response along with that to which he responds. Boys who have read only a few books in their lives, but a great many comic books, will tell one, so vividly that it is easy to sympathize: "I don't like books because they don't really show you things; they're too slow; you have to do all the work yourself." When, in a few years, one talks to boys who have read only a few comic books, but have looked at a great many television programs— what will *they* say?

On this subject of the obscurity of the poet, of the new world that is taking the place of the old, I have written you a poem— an obscure one. I once encountered, in a book, a house that had a formal garden, an English garden, a kitchen garden, and a cutting garden; through these gardens gentlemen walked in silk stockings, their calves padded like those of Mephistopheles; and I made that cutting garden, those padded calves, my symbols for the past. For the present and the future I had so many symbols I didn't know what to do: they came into the poem without knocking, judged it, and did not leave when they had judged; but the one that summed them all up—that had, for me, the sound of the Last Morning of Judgment—was a slogan from a wine-advertisement, one that I used to see every day in the New York subways. My poem is called "The Times Worsen":

> *If sixteen shadows flapping on the line*
> *All sleek with bluing—a Last Morning's wash—*
> *Whistle, "Now that was thoughty, Mrs. Bean,"*
> *I tell myself, I try: A dream, a dream.*
> *But my plaid spectacles are matt as gouache;*
> *When, Sundays, I have finished all the funnies,*
> *I have not finished all the funnies. Men*
> *Walk in all day (to try me) without knocking—*
> *My jurors: these just, vulgar, friendly shades.*
> *The cutting garden of my grandmama,*
> *My great-great-great-grandfather's padded calves*
> *(Greeted, at cockcrow, with the soft small smile*
> *Of Lilith, his first morganatic wife)*
> *Are only a tale from E. T. W. Hoffmann.*
> *When Art goes, what remains is Life.*
> *The World of the Future does not work by halves:*
> *Life is that "wine like Mother used to make—*
> *So rich you can almost cut it with a knife."*

The World of the Future! That world where vegetables are either frozen, canned, or growing in the fields; where little children, as they gaze into the television viewplate at the Babes dead under the heaped-up leaves of the Wood, ask pleadingly: "But where was their electric blanket?"; where old books, hollowed-out to hold fudge, grace every coffee-table; where cavemen in grammar school pageants, clad in pelts of raw cotton, are watched by families dressed entirely—except for the

Neolite of their shoe-soles—in rayon, cellulose, and spun nylon; where, among the related radiances of a kitchen's white-enamelled electric stove, electric dish-washer, electric refrigerator, electric washing-machine, electric dryer, electric ironer, disposal unit, air conditioner, and Waring Blendor, the home-maker sits in the trim coveralls of her profession; where, above the concrete cavern that holds a General Staff, the rockets are invisible in the sky . . . Of this world I often think.

I do not know whether, at this point, any of my hearers will feel like saying to me, "But all this is Negative. What do you want us to *do* about all this?" If I have sounded certain about "all this," let me apologize: these are conclusions which I have come to slowly and reluctantly, as the world forced them on me. Would that I were one of those happy reactionaries, born with a Greek vocabulary as other children are born with birthmarks or incomes, who at the age of four refuse indignantly to waste on that "humanitarian phantasy of a sentimental liberalism, the Kindergarten," the hours they instead devote to memorizing their catechism! But I had a scientific education and a radical youth; am old-fashioned enough to believe, like Goethe, in Progress—the progress I see and the progress I wish for and do not see. So I say what I have said about the poet, the public, and their world angrily and unwillingly. If my hearers say, "But what should we do?" what else can I answer but "Nothing"? There is nothing to do different from what we already do: if poets write poems and readers read them, each as best they can —if they try to live not as soldiers or voters or intellectuals or economic men, but as human beings—they are doing all that can be done. But to expect them (by, say, reciting one-syllable

poems over the radio) to bring back that Yesterday in which
people stood on chairs to look at Lord Tennyson, is to believe
that General Motors can bring back "the tradition of craftsmanship" by giving, as it does, prizes to Boy Scouts for their scale-
models of Napoleonic coaches; to believe that the manners of
the past can be restored by encouraging country-people to say
Grüss Gott or *Howdy, stranger* to the tourists they meet along
summer lanes.

Art matters not merely because it is the most magnificent
ornament and the most nearly unfailing occupation of our lives,
but because it is life itself. From Christ to Freud we have believed that, if we know the truth, the truth will set us free: art is
indispensable because so much of this truth can be learned
through works of art and through works of art alone—for which
of us could have learned for himself what Proust and Chekhov,
Hardy and Yeats and Rilke, Shakespeare and Homer learned
for us? and in what other way could they have made us see the
truths which they themselves saw, those differing and contradictory truths which seem nevertheless, to the mind which
contains them, in some sense a single truth? And all these things,
by their very nature, demand to be shared; if we are satisfied to
know these things ourselves, and to look with superiority or indifference at those who do not have that knowledge, we have
made a refusal that corrupts us as surely as anything can. If
while most of our people (the descendants of those who, ordinarily, listened to Grimm's Tales and the ballads and the
Bible; who, exceptionally, listened to Aeschylus and Shakespeare) listen not to simple or naive art, but to an elaborate and
sophisticated substitute for art, an immediate and infallible

synthetic as effective and terrifying as advertisements or the speeches of Hitler—if, knowing all this, we say: *Art has always been a matter of a few*, we are using a truism to hide a disaster. One of the oldest, deepest, and most nearly conclusive attractions of democracy is manifested in our feeling that through it not only material but also spiritual goods can be shared: that in a democracy bread and justice, education and art, will be accessible to everybody. If a democracy should offer its citizens a show of education, a sham art, a literacy more dangerous than their old illiteracy, then we should have to say that it is not a democracy at all, but one more variant of those "People's Democracies" which share with any true democracy little more than the name. Goethe said: The only way in which we can come to terms with the great superiority of another person is love. But we can also come to terms with superiority, with true Excellence, by denying that such a thing as Excellence can exist; and, in doing so, we help to destroy it and ourselves.

I was sorry to see this conference given its (quite traditional) name of The Defense of Poetry. Poetry does not need to be defended, any more than air or food needs to be defended; poetry—using the word in its widest sense, the only sense in which it is important—has been an indispensable part of any culture we know anything about. Human life without some form of poetry is not human life but animal existence. Our world today is not an impossible one for poets and poetry: poets can endure its disadvantages, and good poetry is still being written —Yeats, for instance, thought the first half of this century the greatest age of lyric poetry since the Elizabethan. But what will happen to the public—to that portion of it divorced from any real art even of the simplest kind—I do not know. Yet an analogy occurs to me.

One sees, in the shops of certain mountainous regions of Austria, bands of silver links, clasped like necklaces, which have at the front jeweled or enameled silver plates, sometimes quite large ones. These pieces of jewelry are called *goiter-bands:* they are ornaments which in the past were used to adorn a woman's diseased, enormously swollen neck. If the women who wore them could have been told that they had been made hideous by the lack of an infinitesimal proportion of iodine in the water of the mountain valley in which they lived, they would have laughed at the notion. They would have laughed even more heartily at the notion that their necks *were* hideous—and their lovers would have asked, as they looked greedily at the round flesh under the flaxen pigtails, how anyone could bear to caress the poor, thin, scrawny, chickenish necks of those other women they now and then saw, foreigners from that flatland which travellers call the world.

I have talked about the poet and his public; but who is his public, really? In a story by E. M. Forster called *The Machine Stops*, there is a conversation between a mother and her son. They are separated by half the circumference of the earth; they sit under the surface of the earth in rooms supplied with air, with food, and with warmth as automatically as everything else is supplied to these people of the far future. "Imagine," as Forster says, "a swaddled lump of flesh—a woman, about five feet high, with a face as white as a fungus." She has just refused to go to visit her son; she has no time. Her son replies:

"The air-ship barely takes two days to fly between me and you."

"I dislike air-ships."

"Why?"

"I dislike seeing the horrible brown earth, and the sea, and the stars when it is dark. I get no ideas in an air-ship."

"I do not get them anywhere else."

"What kind of ideas can the air give you?"

He paused for an instant.

"Do you not know four big stars that form an oblong, and three stars close together in the middle of the oblong, and hanging from these stars, three other stars?"

"No, I do not. I dislike the stars. But did they give you an idea? How interesting; tell me."

"I had an idea that they were like a man."

"I do not understand."

"The four big stars are the man's shoulders and his knees. The three stars in the middle are like the belts that men wore once, and the three stars hanging are like a sword."

"A sword?"

"Men carried swords about with them, to kill animals and other men."

"It does not strike me as a very good idea, but it is certainly original."

As long as these stars remain in this shape; as long as there is a man left to look at them and to discover that they are the being Orion: for at least this long the poet will have his public. And when this man too is gone, and neither the poems, the poet, nor the public exist any longer—and this possibility can no longer seem to us as strange as it would once have seemed— there is surely some order of the world, some level of being, at which they still subsist: an order in which the lost plays of Aeschylus are no different from those that have been preserved, an order in which the past, the present, and the future have in some sense the same reality. Or so—whether we think so or not— so we all feel. People always ask: *For whom does the poet write?* He needs only to answer, *For whom do you do good? Are you kind to your daughter because in the end someone will pay you for being?* . . . The poet writes his poem for its own sake, for the sake of that order of things in which the poem takes the place that has awaited it.

But this has been said, better than it is ever again likely to be said, by the greatest of the writers of this century, Marcel Proust; and I should like to finish this lecture by quoting his sentences:

"All that we can say is that everything is arranged in this life as though we entered it carrying the burden of obligations contracted in a former life; there is no reason inherent in the conditions of life on this earth that can make us consider ourselves obliged to do good, to be fastidious, to be polite even, nor make the talented artist consider himself obliged to begin over again a score of times a piece of work the admiration aroused by which will matter little to his body devoured by worms, like the patch of yellow wall painted with so much knowledge and skill by an artist who must for ever remain unknown and is barely identified under the name Vermeer. All these obligations which have not their sanction in our present life seem to belong to a different world, founded upon kindness, scrupulosity, self-sacrifice, a world entirely different from this, which we leave in order to be born into this world, before perhaps returning to the other to live once again beneath the sway of those unknown laws which we have obeyed because we bore their precepts in our hearts, knowing not whose hand had traced them there—those laws to which every profound work of the intellect brings us nearer and which are invisible only— and still!—to fools."

The Other Frost

BESIDES the Frost that everybody knows there is one whom no one even talks about. Everybody knows what the regular Frost is: the one living poet who has written *good* poems that ordinary readers like without any trouble and understand without any trouble; the conservative editorialist and self-made apothegm-joiner, full of dry wisdom and free, complacent, Yankee enterprise; the Farmer-Poet—this is an imposing private rôle perfected for public use, a sort of Olympian Will Rogers out of *Tanglewood Tales;* and, last or first of all, Frost is the standing, speaking reproach to any other good modern poet: "If Frost can write poetry that's just as easy as Longfellow you can too—you do too." It is this "easy" side of Frost that is most attractive to academic readers, who are eager to canonize any modern poet who condemns in example the modern poetry which they condemn in precept; and it is this side that has helped to get him neglected or depreciated by intellectuals—the reader of Eliot or Auden usually dismisses Frost as something inconsequentially good that *he* knew all about long ago. Ordinary readers think Frost the greatest poet alive, and love some of his best poems almost as much as they love some of his worst ones. He seems to them a sensible, tender, humorous poet who knows all about trees and farms and folks in New England, and still has managed to get an individualistic, fairly optimistic, thoroughly American philosophy out of what he knows; there's something reassuring about his poetry, they feel—almost like prose. Certainly there's nothing hard or odd or gloomy about it.

These views of Frost, it seems to me, come either from not knowing his poems well enough or from knowing the wrong poems too well. Frost's best-known poems, with a few exceptions, are not his best poems at all; when you read (say) the selections in Untermeyer, you are getting a good synopsis of the ordinary idea of Frost and a bad misrepresentation of the real Frost. It would be hard to make a novel list of Eliot's best poems, but one can make a list of ten or twelve of Frost's best poems that is likely to seem to anybody too new to be true. Here it is: "The Witch of Coös," "Neither Out Far Nor In Deep," "Directive," "Design," "A Servant to Servants," "Provide Provide," "Home-Burial," "Acquainted with the Night," "The Pauper Witch of Grafton" (mainly for its ending), "An Old Man's Winter Night," "The Gift Outright," "After Apple-Picking," "Desert Places," and "The Fear."

Nothing I say about these poems can make you see what they are like, or what the Frost that matters most is like; if you read them you will see. "The Witch of Coös" is the best thing of its kind since Chaucer. "Home-Burial" and "A Servant to Servants" are two of the most moving and appalling dramatic

29

poems ever written; and how could lyrics be more ingeniously and conclusively merciless than "Neither Out Far Nor In Deep" or "Design"? or more grotesquely and subtly and mercilessly disenchanting than the tender "An Old Man's Winter Night"? or more unsparingly truthful than "Provide Provide"? And so far from being obvious, optimistic, orthodox, many of these poems are extraordinarily subtle and strange, poems which express an attitude that, at its most extreme, makes pessimism seem a hopeful evasion; they begin with a flat and terrible reproduction of the evil in the world and end by saying: It's so; and there's nothing you can do about it; and if there were, would *you* ever do it? The limits which existence approaches and falls back from have seldom been stated with such bare composure.

Frost's virtues are extraordinary. No other living poet has written so well about the actions of ordinary men: his wonderful dramatic monologues or dramatic scenes come out of a knowledge of people that few poets have had, and they are written in a verse that uses, sometimes with absolute mastery, the rhythms of actual speech. Particularly in his blank verse there is a movement so characteristic, so unmistakably and overwhelmingly Frost's, that one feels about it almost as Madame de Guermantes felt about those Frans Halses at Haarlem: that if you caught just a glimpse of them, going by in the street-car, you would be able to tell they were something pretty unusual. It is easy to underestimate the effect of this exact, spaced-out, prosaic rhythm, whose objects have the tremendous strength—you find it in Hardy's best poems—of things merely put down and left to speak for themselves. (Though Frost has little of Hardy's self-effacement, his matter-of-fact humility; Frost's tenderness, sadness, and humor are adulterated with vanity and a hard complacency.) Frost's seriousness and honesty; the bare sorrow with which, sometimes, things are accepted as they are, neither exaggerated nor explained away; the many, many poems in which there are real people with their real speech and real thoughts and real emotions—all this, in conjunction with so much subtlety and exactness, such classical understatement and restraint, makes the reader feel that he is not in a book but in a world, and a world that has in common with his own some of the things that are most important in both. I don't need to praise anything so justly famous as Frost's observation of and empathy with everything in Nature from a hornet to a hillside; and he has observed his own nature, one person's random or consequential chains of thoughts and feelings and perceptions, quite as well. (And this person, in the poems, is not the "alienated artist" cut off from everybody who isn't, yum-yum, another alienated artist; he is someone like normal people only more so—a normal person in the less common and more important sense of *normal*.) The least crevice of the good poems is saturated with imagination, an imagination that expresses itself in the continual wit and humor and particularity of what is said, in the hand-hewn or hand-polished texture of its saying. The responsibility and seriousness of Frost's best work—his worst work has an irresponsible conceit, an indifference to everything but himself, that appalls one—are nowhere better manifested than in the organization of these poems: an organization that, in its concern for any involution or ramification that really belongs to its subject, and in its severity toward anything else, expresses that absorption into a subject that is prior even to affection. The organization of Frost's poems is often rather simple or—as people say—"old-fashioned." But, as people ought to know, very complicated organizations are excessively rare in poetry, although in our time a very complicated disorganization has been excessively common; there is more successful organization in "Home-Burial" or "The Witch of Coös"—one feels like saying, in indignant exaggeration—than in the *Cantos* and *The Bridge* put together. These titles will remind anyone of what is scarcest in Frost: rhetoric and romance, hypnotic verbal excitement, Original Hart Crane. Frost's word-magic is generally of a quiet, sober, bewitching sort, though the contrasts he gets from his greyed or unsaturated shades are often more satisfying to a thoughtful rhetorician than some dazzling arrangements of prismatic colors. Yet there are dazzling passages in Frost.

Frost has written, as everybody knows: "I never dared be radical when young/ For fear it would make me conservative when old." This is about as truthful as it is metrical: Frost *was* radical when young—he was a very odd and very radical radical, a much more interesting sort than the standard *New Republic* brand—and now that he's old he's sometimes callously and unimaginatively conservative. Take his poems about the atomic bomb in *Steeple Bush;* these amount, almost, to a very old and a very successful man saying: "I've had my life—why should you worry about yours?" The man who called himself "the author/ Of several books against the world in general"; who said that he had learned from Marlowe's Mephistopheles to say his prayers, "Why this is Hell, nor am I out of it"; who said to Henry Hudson, drowned or frozen somewhere in Hudson's Bay: "You and I and the Great Auk"; who could be annoyed at a hornet for not recognizing him as "the exception I like to think I am in everything"; who in poems like "A Servant to Servants," "Home-Burial," and "The Witch of Coös" had a final identifying knowledge of the deprived and dispossessed, the insulted and injured, that one matches in modern poetry only in Hardy —this poet is now, most of the time, an elder statesman like Baruch or Smuts, full of complacent wisdom and cast-iron whimsy. But of course there was always a good deal of this in the official rôle that Frost created for himself; one imagines Yeats saying about Frost, as Sarah Bernhardt said about Nijinsky: "I fear, I greatly fear, that I have just seen the greatest actor in the world."

Sometimes it is this public figure, this official rôle—the Only Genuine Robert Frost in Captivity—that writes the poems, and not the poet himself; and then one gets a self-made man's political editorials, full of cracker-box philosophizing, almanac joke-cracking—of a snake-oil salesman's mysticism; one gets the public figure's relishing consciousness of himself, an astonishing constriction of imagination and sympathy; one gets sentimentality and whimsicality, an arch complacency, a complacent archness; and one gets Homely Wisdom till the cows come home. Often the later Frost makes demands on himself that are minimal: he uses a little wit and a little observation and a little sentiment to stuff—not very tight—a little sonnet; and it's not bad, but not good enough to matter, either. The extremely rare, extremely wonderful dramatic and narrative element that is more important than anything else in his early poetry almost disappears from his later poetry; in his later work the best

33

poems are usually special-case, rather than all-out, full-scale affairs. The younger Frost is surrounded by his characters, living beings he has known or created; the older Frost is alone. But it is this loneliness that is responsible for the cold finality of poems like "Neither Out Far Nor In Deep" or "Design."

Frost's latest books deserve little more than a footnote, since they have had few of his virtues, most of his vices, and all of his tricks; the heathen who would be converted to Frost by them is hard to construct. *Steeple Bush* has one wonderful poem, "Directive"; a fairly good, dazzlingly heartless one, "The Ingenuities of Debt"; and nothing else that is not done better somewhere else in Frost. Most of the poems merely remind you, by their persistence in the mannerisms of what was genius, that they are the productions of someone who once, and somewhere else, was a great poet. But one stops for a long time at "Directive."

A Masque of Mercy, though no great shakes—as you see, its style is catching—is a great improvement on the earlier *A Masque of Reason*, which is a frivolous, trivial, and bewilderingly corny affair, full of jokes inexplicable except as the contemptuous patter of an old magician certain that *he* can get away with anything in the world: *What fools these readers be!* Besides, Frost has long ago divorced reason for common sense, and is basking complacently in his bargain; consequently, when common sense has God justify His ways to Job by saying, "I was just showing off to Satan," the performance has the bleak wisdom of Calvin Coolidge telling you what life comes to at $2\frac{1}{2}\%$.

The plot of *A Masque of Mercy* is as simple as that of *Merope*, but it is a plot that is more likely to get Frost recognized as one more precursor of surrealism than it is to get him looked askance at as one of Arnold's Greeks. A bookstore-keeper named My Brother's Keeper has a wife named Jesse Bel; one night Jonah— who, having forgotten both his gourd and what God taught him by it, is feeling for New York City all the hatred that he used to feel for Nineveh—seeks refuge in the bookstore; after a little talk from Saint Paul (Jesse Bel's psychiatrist) and a lot of talk from Keeper (a character who develops so much that he finally develops into Robert Frost), Jonah comes to realize that "justice doesn't really matter."

Frost lavishes some care and a good deal more self-indulgence on this congenial subject. He has a thorough skepticism about that tame revenge, justice, and a cold certainty that nothing but mercy will do for *us*. What he really warms to is a rejection beyond either justice or mercy, and the most felt and moving part of his poem is the "unshaken recognition"—that is to say, the willing assertion—that

> *Our sacrifice, the best we have to offer,*
> *And not our worst nor second best, our best,*
> *Our very best, our lives laid down like Jonah's,*
> *Our lives laid down in war and peace, may not*
> *Be found acceptable in Heaven's sight.*

To feel this Fear of God and to go ahead in spite of it, Frost says, is man's principal virtue, courage. He treats Paul very sympathetically, but gives him speeches that are ineffectual echoes of what he really said; and Frost makes about him that sorry old joke which finds that he "theologized Christ out of Christianity." Paul ends in jokes like this, Columbus in chains; these are the rewards of discovery.

To the Laodiceans

BACK in the days when "serious readers of modern poetry" were most patronizing to Frost's poems, one was often moved to argument, or to article-writing, or to saying under one's breath: *What is man that Thou art mindful of him?* In these days it's better—a little, not much: the lips are pursed that ought to be parted, and they still pay lip-service, or little more. But Frost's best poetry—and there is a great deal of it, at once wonderfully different and wonderfully alike—deserves the attention, submission, and astonished awe that real art always requires of us; to give it a couple of readings and a ribbon lettered First in the Old-Fashioned (or Before 1900) Class of Modern Poetry is worse, almost, than not to read it at all. Surely *we* [I don't know exactly whom this *we* includes, but perhaps I could say that it means "the friends of things in the spirit," even when the things are difficult, even when the things are in the flesh] are not going to be like the *Saturday Review* readers and writers who tell one how completely good Frost is, and in the next breath tell one how narrowly good, limitedly good, badly good Eliot is. Surely it is the excellence most unlike our own that we will be most eager to acknowledge, since it not only extends but completes us—and since only we, not the excellence, are harmed by our rejection of it.

Frost has limitations of a kind very noticeable to us, but they are no more important than those of other contemporary poets; and most of the limitations, less noticeable to us, that these poets share, Frost is free of. If it makes good sense (but a narrow and ungenerous, though essential, sense) to say about Frost, "As a poet he isn't in Rilke's class at all," it does *not* make such sense if you substitute for Rilke's name that of Eliot or Moore or Stevens or Auden, that of any living poet. We can already see, most vividly, how ridiculous posterity is going to find the people who thought Marianne Moore's poems "not poetry at all," *The Waste Land* a hoax, and so on; but is posterity going to find any less ridiculous the intellectuals who admitted Frost only as a second-class citizen of the Republic of Letters, a "bard" whom it would be absurd to compare with real modern poets like—oh, E. E. Cummings? Frost's daemonic gift of always getting on the buttered side of both God and Mammon; of doing and saying anything and everything that he pleases, and still getting the World to approve or tactfully ignore every bit of it; of not only allowing, but taking a hard pleasure in encouraging, fools and pedants to adore him as their own image magnified—all this has helped to keep us from seeing Frost for what he really is. And here one has no right to be humble and agreeable, and to concede beforehand that *what he really is* is only one's own "view" or "interpretation" of him: the regular ways of looking at Frost's poetry are grotesque simplifications, distortions, falsifications—coming to know his poetry well ought to be enough, in itself, to dispel any of them, and to make plain the necessity of finding some other way of talking about his work.

Any of us but Frost himself (and all the little Frostlings who sit round him wondering with a foolish face of praise, dealing out ten monosyllables to the homey line) can by now afford just to wonder at his qualities, not to sadden at his defects, and can gladly risk looking a little foolish in the process. The real complication, sophistication, and ambiguity of Frost's thought [what poet since Arnold has written so much about isolation, and said so much more about it than even Arnold? what other poet, long before we had begun to perfect the means of altogether doing away with humanity, had taken as an obsessive subject the wiping-out of man, his replacement by the nature out of which he arose?], the range and depth and height of his poems, have had justice done to them by neither his admirers nor his detractors—and, alas, aren't going to have justice done to them by me now. If one is talking about Frost's poetry to friends, or giving a course in it to students, one can go over thirty or forty of his best poems and feel sure about everything: one doesn't need, then, to praise or blame or generalize—the poems speak for themselves almost as well as poems can. But when one writes a little article about Frost, one feels lamentably sure of how lamentably short of his world the article is going to fall; one can never write about him without wishing that it were a whole book, a book in which one could talk about hundreds of poems and hundreds of other things, and fall short by one's essential and not accidental limitations.

I have sometimes written, and often talked, about Frost's willful, helpless, all too human mixture of virtues and vices, so I hope that this time I will be allowed simply—in the nice, old-fashioned, looked-down-on phrase—to appreciate. And I want to appreciate more than his best poems, I want to exclaim over some of the unimportantly delightful and marvellously characteristic ones, and over some of the places where all of Frost and all of what is being described are married and indistinguishable in one line. But first let me get rid, in a few sentences, of that Skeleton on the Doorstep that is the joy of his enemies and the despair of his friends. Just as a star will have, sometimes, a dark companion, so Frost has a pigheaded one, a shadowy self that grows longer and darker as the sun gets lower. I am speaking of that other self that might be called the Grey Eminence of Robert Taft, or the Peter Pan of the National Association of Manufacturers, or any such thing—this public self incarnates all the institutionalized complacency that Frost once mocked at and fled from, and later pretended to become a part of and became a part of. This Yankee Editorialist side of Frost gets in the way of *everything*—of us, of the real Frost, of the real poems and their real subject-matter. And a poet so magically good at making the subtlest of points surely shouldn't evolve into one who regularly comes out and tells you the point after it's been made—and comes out and tells you, in such trudging doctrinaire lines, a point like the end of a baseball bat. Frost says in a piece of homely doggerel that he has hoped wisdom could be not only Attic but Laconic, Boeotian even— "at least not systematic"; but how systematically Frostian the worst of his later poems are! His good poems are the best refutation of, the most damning comment on, his bad: his *Complete Poems* have the air of being able to educate any faithful reader into tearing out a third of the pages, reading a third, and practically wearing out the rest.

We begin to read Frost, always, with the taste of "Birches" in our mouth—a taste a little brassy, a little sugary; and to take it out I will use not such good and familiar poems as "Mending Wall" and "After Apple-Picking," or such a wonderful and familiar (and misunderstood) poem as "An Old Man's Winter Night," but four or five of Frost's best and least familiar poems. Let me begin with a poem that, at first glance, hardly seems a Frost poem at all, but reminds us more of another kind of unfamiliar poem that Housman wrote; this poem is called "Neither Out Far Nor In Deep":

The people along the sand
All turn and look one way.
They turn their back on the land.
They look at the sea all day.

As long as it takes to pass
A ship keeps raising its hull;
The wetter ground like glass
Reflects a standing gull.

The land may vary more;
But wherever the truth may be—
The water comes ashore,
And the people look at the sea.

> *They cannot look out far.*
> *They cannot look in deep.*
> *But when was that ever a bar*
> *To any watch they keep?*

First of all, of course, the poem is simply there, in indifferent unchanging actuality; but our thought about it, what we are made to make of it, is there too, made to be there. When we choose between land and sea, the human and the inhuman, the finite and the infinite, the sea *has* to be the infinite that floods in over us endlessly, the hypnotic monotony of the universe that is incommensurable with us—everything into which we look neither very far nor very deep, but look, look just the same. And yet Frost doesn't say so—it is the geometry of this very geometrical poem, its inescapable structure, that says so. There is the deepest tact and restraint in the symbolism; it is like Housman's

> *Stars, I have seen them fall,*
> *But when they drop and die*
> *No star is lost at all*
> *From all the star-sown sky.*
>
> *The toil of all that be*
> *Helps not the primal fault:*
> *It rains into the sea*
> *And still the sea is salt.*

But Frost's poem is flatter, greyer, and at once tenderer and more terrible, without even the consolations of rhetoric and exaggeration—there is no "primal fault" in Frost's poem, but only the faint Biblical memories of "any watch they keep." What we do know we don't care about; what we do care about we don't know: we can't look out very far, or in very deep; and when did that ever bother *us*? It would be hard to find anything more unpleasant to say about people than that last stanza; but Frost doesn't say it unpleasantly—he says it with flat ease, takes everything with something harder than contempt, more passive than acceptance. And isn't there something heroic about the whole business, too—something touching about our absurdity? if the fool persisted in his folly he would become a wise man, Blake said, and we have persisted. The tone of the last lines—or, rather, their careful suspension between several tones, as a piece of iron can be held in the air between powerful enough magnets—allows for this too. This recognition of the essential limitations of man, without denial or protest or rhetoric or palliation, is very rare and very valuable, and rather usual in Frost's best poetry. One is reminded of Empson's thoughtful and truthful comment on Gray's "Elegy": "Many people, without being communists, have been irritated by the complacence in the massive calm of the poem . . . And yet what is said is one of the permanent truths; it is only in degree that any improvement of society would prevent wastage of human powers; the waste even in a fortunate life, the isolation even of a life rich in intimacy, cannot but be felt deeply, and is the central feeling of tragedy."

Another of Frost's less familiar poems is called "Provide Provide":

43

The witch that came (the withered hag)
To wash the steps with pail and rag
Was once the beauty Abishag,

The picture pride of Hollywood.
Too many fall from great and good
For you to doubt the likelihood.

Die early and avoid the fate.
Or if predestined to die late,
Make up your mind to die in state.

Make the whole stock exchange your own!
If need be occupy a throne,
Where nobody can call you crone.

Some have relied on what they knew;
Others on being simply true.
What worked for them might work for you.

No memory of having starred
Atones for later disregard
Or keeps the end from being hard.

Better to go down dignified
With boughten friendship at your side
Than none at all. Provide, provide!

For many readers this poem will need no comment at all, and
for others it will need rather more than I could ever give. The
poem is—to put it as crudely as possible—an immortal masterpiece; and if we murmur something about its crudities and pro-

vincialisms, History will smile tenderly at us and lay us in the corner beside those cultivated people from Oxford and Cambridge who thought Shakespeare a Hollywood scenario-writer. Since I can't write five or six pages about the poem, it might be better to say only that it is full of the deepest, and most touching, moral wisdom—and it is full, too, of the life we have to try to be wise about and moral in (the sixth stanza is almost unbearably actual). The Wisdom of this World and the wisdom that comes we know not whence exist together in the poem, not side by side but one inside the other; yet the whole poem exists for, lives around, the fifth stanza and its *others on being simply true*—was restraint ever more moving? One can quote about that line Rilke's *In the end the only defence is defencelessness*, and need to say no more. But the rest of the poem is the more that we need to say, if we decide to say any more: it says, in the worldliest and homeliest of terms, that expediency won't work—the poem is, even in its form, a marvellous *reductio ad absurdum* of expediency—but since you *will* try it, since you *will* provide for the morrow, then provide hard for it, be really expedient, settle yourself for life in the second-best bed around which the heirs gather, the very best second-best bed. The poem is so particularly effective because it is the Wisdom of this World which demonstrates to us that the Wisdom of this World isn't enough. The poem puts, so to speak, the minimal case for morality, and then makes the minimal recommendation of it (*what worked for them might work for you*); but this has a beauty and conclusiveness that aren't minimal.

The most awful of Frost's smaller poems is one called "Design":

45

I found a dimpled spider, fat and white,
On a white heal-all, holding up a moth
Like a white piece of rigid satin cloth—
Assorted characters of death and blight
Mixed ready to begin the morning right,
Like the ingredients of a witch's broth—
A snow-drop spider, a flower like froth,
And dead wings carried like a paper kite.

What had that flower to do with being white,
The wayside blue and innocent heal-all?
What brought the kindred spider to that height,
Then steered the white moth thither in the night?
What but design of darkness to appall?—
If design govern in a thing so small.

This is the Argument from Design with a vengeance; is the terrible negative from which the eighteenth century's Kodak picture (with its *Having wonderful time. Wish you were here* on the margin) had to be printed. If a watch, then a watch-maker; if a diabolical machine, then a diabolical mechanic—Frost uses exactly the logic that has always been used. And this little albino catastrophe is too whitely catastrophic to be accidental, too impossibly unlikely ever to be a coincidence: accident, chance, statistics, natural selection are helpless to account for such designed terror and heartbreak, such an awful symbolic perversion of the innocent being of the world. Frost's details are so diabolically good that it seems criminal to leave some unremarked; but notice how *dimpled, fat,* and *white* (all but one; all but one) come from our regular description of any baby;

notice how the *heal-all*, because of its name, is the one flower in all the world picked to be the altar for this Devil's Mass; notice how *holding up* the moth brings something ritual and hieratic, a ghostly, ghastly formality, to this priest and its sacrificial victim; notice how terrible to the fingers, how full of the stilling rigor of death, that *white piece of rigid satin cloth* is. And *assorted characters of death and blight* is, like so many things in this poem, sharply ambiguous: *a mixed bunch of actors* or *diverse representative signs.* The tone of the phrase *assorted characters of death and blight* is beautifully developed in the ironic Breakfast-Club-calisthenics, Radio-Kitchen heartiness of *mixed ready to begin the morning right* (which assures us, so unreassuringly, that this isn't any sort of Strindberg *Spook Sonata*, but hard fact), and concludes in the *ingredients* of the witch's broth, giving the soup a sort of cuddly shimmer that the cauldron in *Macbeth* never had; the *broth*, even, is brought to life—we realize that witch's broth *is* broth, to be supped with a long spoon. For sweet-sour, smiling awfulness *snow-drop spider* looks unsurpassable, until we come to the almost obscenely horrible (even the mouth-gestures are utilized) *a flower like froth;* this always used to seem to me the case of the absolutely inescapable effect, until a student of mine said that you could tell how beautiful the flower was because the poet compared it to froth; when I said to her, "But—but—but what does froth *remind* you of?" looking desperately into her blue eyes, she replied: "Fudge. It reminds me of making fudge."

And then, in the victim's own little line, how contradictory and awful everything is: *dead wings carried like a paper kite!* The *dead* and the *wings* work back and forth on each other heartbreakingly, and the contradictory pathos of the *carried* wings is exceeded by that of the matter-of-fact conversion into what has never lived, into a shouldered toy, of the ended life. *What had that flower to do with being white,/ The wayside blue and innocent heal-all?* expresses as well as anything ever has the arbitrariness of our guilt, the fact that Original Sin is only Original Accident, so far as the creatures of this world are concerned. And *the wayside blue and innocent heal-all* is, down to the least sound, the last helpless, yearning, trailing-away sigh of too-precarious innocence, of a potentiality cancelled out almost before it began to exist. The *wayside* makes it universal, commonplace, and somehow dearer to us; the *blue* brings in all the associations of the normal negated color (the poem is likely to remind the reader of Melville's chapter on the Whiteness of the Whale, just as Frost may have been reminded); and the *innocent* is given a peculiar force and life by this context, just as the name *heal-all* here comes to sad, ironic, literal life: it healed all, itself it could not heal. The *kindred* is very moving in its half-forgiving ambiguity; and the Biblical *thither in the night* and the conclusive *steered* (with its careful echoes of "To a Water-Fowl" and a thousand sermons) are very moving and very serious in their condemnation, their awful mystery. The partly ambiguous, summing-up *What but design of darkness to appall* comes as something taken for granted, a relief almost, in its mere statement and generalization, after the almost unbearable actuality and particularity of what has come before. And then this whole appalling categorical machinery of reasoning-out, of conviction, of condemnation—it reminds one of the machine in *The Penal*

Colony—is suddenly made merely hypothetical, a possible contradicted shadow, by one off-hand last-minute qualification:
one that dismisses it, but that dismisses it only for a possibility
still more terrifying, a whole new random, statistical, astronomical abyss underlying the diabolical machinery of the poem.
"In large things, macroscopic phenomena of some real importance," the poem says, "the classical mechanics of design
probably *does* operate—though in reverse, so far as the old
Argument from Design is concerned; but these little things,
things of no real importance, microscopic phenomena like a
flower or moth or man or planet or solar system [we have so
indissolubly identified ourselves with the moth and flower and
spider that we cannot treat our own nature and importance,
which theirs symbolize, as fundamentally different from theirs],
are governed by the purely statistical laws of quantum mechanics, of random distribution, are they not?" I have given
this statement of "what the poem says"—it says much more—
an exaggeratedly physical, scientific form because both a
metaphorically and literally astronomical view of things is so
common, and so unremarked-on, in Frost. This poem, I think
most people will admit, makes Pascal's "eternal silence of those
infinite spaces" seem the hush between the movements of a
cantata.

Another impressive unfamiliar poem is "The Most of It,"
a poem which indicates as well as any I can think of Frost's
stubborn truthfulness, his willingness to admit both the falseness in the cliché and the falseness in the contradiction of the
cliché; if the universe never gives us either a black or a white

answer, but only a black-and-white one that is somehow not an answer at all, still its inhuman not-answer exceeds any answer that we human beings could have thought of or wished for:

> *He thought he kept the universe alone;*
> *For all the voice in answer he could wake*
> *Was but the mocking echo of his own*
> *From some tree-hidden cliff across the lake.*
> *Some morning from the boulder-broken beach*
> *He would cry out on life, that what it wants*
> *Is not its own love back in copy speech,*
> *But counter-love, original response.*
> *And nothing ever came of what he crie,*
> *Unless it was the embodiment that crashed*
> *In the cliff's talus on the other side,*
> *And then in the far distant water splashed,*
> *But after a time allowed for it to swim,*
> *Instead of proving human when it neared*
> *And someone else additional to him,*
> *As a great buck it powerfully appeared,*
> *Pushing the crumpled water up ahead,*
> *And landed pouring like a waterfall,*
> *And stumbled through the rocks with horny tread,*
> *And forced the underbrush—and that was all.*

But one of the strangest and most characteristic, most dismaying and most gratifying, poems any poet has ever written is a poem called "Directive." It shows the coalescence of three of Frost's obsessive themes, those of isolation, of extinction,

and of the final limitations of man—is Frost's last word about
all three:

> Back out of all this now too much for us,
> Back in a time made simple by the loss
> Of detail, burned, dissolved, and broken off
> Like graveyard marble sculpture in the weather,
> There is a house that is no more a house
> Upon a farm that is no more a farm
> And in a town that is no more a town.
> The road there, if you'll let a guide direct you
> Who only has at heart your getting lost,
> May seem as if it should have been a quarry—
> Great monolithic knees the former town
> Long since gave up pretence of keeping covered.
> And there's a story in a book about it:
> Besides the wear of iron wagon wheels
> The ledges show lines ruled southeast northwest,
> The chisel work of an enormous Glacier
> That braced his feet against the Arctic Pole.
> You must not mind a certain coolness from him
> Still said to haunt this side of Panther Mountain.
> Nor need you mind the serial ordeal
> Of being watched from forty cellar holes
> As if by eye pairs out of forty firkins.
> As for the wood's excitement over you
> That sends light rustle rushes to their leaves,
> Charge that to upstart inexperience.

Where were they all not twenty years ago?
They think too much of having shaded out
A few old pecker-fretted apple trees.
Make yourself up a cheering song of how
Someone's road home from work this once was,
Who may be just ahead of you on foot
Or creaking with a buggy load of grain.
The height of the adventure is the height
Of country where two village cultures faded
Into each other. Both of them are lost.
And if you're lost enough to find yourself
By now, pull in your ladder road behind you
And put a sign up CLOSED *to all but me.*
Then make yourself at home. The only field
Now left's no bigger than a harness gall.
First there's the children's house of make believe,
Some shattered dishes underneath a pine,
The playthings in the playhouse of the children.
Weep for what little things could make them glad.
Then for the house that is no more a house,
But only a belilaced cellar hole,
Now slowly closing like a dent in dough.
This was no playhouse but a house in earnest.
Your destination and your destiny's
A brook that was the water of the house,
Cold as a spring as yet so near its source,
Too lofty and original to rage.
(We know the valley streams that when aroused

Will leave their tatters hung on barb and thorn.)
I have kept hidden in the instep arch
Of an old cedar at the waterside
A broken drinking goblet like the Grail
Under a spell so the wrong ones can't find it,
So can't get saved, as Saint Mark says they mustn't.
(I stole the goblet from the children's playhouse.)
Here are your waters and your watering place.
Drink and be whole again beyond confusion.

There are weak places in the poem, but these are nothing
beside so much longing, tenderness, and passive sadness, Frost's
understanding that each life is pathetic because it wears away
into the death that it at last half-welcomes—that even its
salvation, far back at the cold root of things, is make-believe,
drunk from a child's broken and stolen goblet, a plaything
hidden among the ruins of the lost cultures. Here the waters of
Lethe are the waters of childhood, and in their depths, with
ambiguous grace, man's end is joined to his beginning. Is the
poem consoling or heart-breaking? Very much of both; and its
humor and acceptance and humanity, its familiarity and
elevation, give it a composed matter-of-fact magnificence. Much
of the strangeness of the poem is far under the surface, or else so
much on the surface, in the subtlest of details (how many readers
will connect the *serial ordeal* of the eye-pairs with the poem's
Grail-parody?), that one slides under it unnoticing. But the
first wonderful sentence; the six lines about the wood's excitement; the knowledge that produces the sentence beginning

53

make yourself up a cheering song; the *both of them are lost;* incidental graces like the *eye-pairs out of forty firkins,* the *harness gall,* the *belilaced cellar-hole* closing *like a dent in dough,* the plays on the word *lost;* the whole description of the children's playhouse, with the mocking (at whom does it mock?) and beautiful *weep for what little things could make them glad;* the grave, terrible *this was no playhouse but a house in earnest;* the four wonderful conclusive sentences—these, and the whole magical and helpless mastery of the poem, are things that many readers have noticed and will notice: the poem is hard to understand, but easy to love.

In another poem Frost worries about the bird that, waked in moonlight, "sang halfway through its little inborn tune," and then he realizes that the bird is as safe as ever, that any increase in danger must necessarily be an infinitesimal one, or else

> *It could not have come down to us so far*
> *Through the interstices of things ajar*
> *On the long bead chain of repeated birth.*

The thought, which would surely have made Darwin give a little gratified smile, might very well have pleased with its "interstices of things ajar" that earlier writer who said, "Absent thee from felicity awhile/ And in this harsh world draw thy breath in pain." For Frost is sometimes a marvellous rhetorician, a writer so completely master of his own rhetorical effects that he can alter both their degree and kind almost as he pleases. In "The Black Cottage" he is able to write the most touchingly and hauntingly prosaic of lines about the passing away of this world:

He fell at Gettysburg or Fredericksburg.
I ought to know—it makes a difference which:
Fredericksburg wasn't Gettysburg, of course . . .

and he is also able to end the poem with the magnificence of

"As I sit here, and oftentimes, I wish
I could be monarch of a desert land
I could devote and dedicate forever
To the truths we keep coming back and back to.
So desert it would have to be, so walled
By mountain ranges half in summer snow,
No one would covet it or think it worth
The pains of conquering to force change on.
Scattered oases where men dwell, but mostly
Sand dunes held loosely in tamarisk
Blown over and over themselves in idleness.
Sand grains should sugar in the natal dew
The babe born to the desert, the sand storm
Retard mid-waste my cowering caravans—
There are bees in this wall." He struck the clapboards,
Fierce heads looked out; small bodies pivoted.
We rose to go. Sunset blazed on the windows.

One sees this extraordinary command in the composed, thoughtful, and traditional rhetoric of "The Gift Outright," one of the best of Frost's smaller poems, and perhaps the best "patriotic" poem ever written about our own country:

The land was ours before we were the land's.
She was our land more than a hundred years
Before we were her people. She was ours

55

In Massachusetts, in Virginia,
But we were England's, still colonials,
Possessing what we still were unpossessed by,
Possessed by what we now no more possessed.
Something we were withholding made us weak
Until we found it was ourselves
We were withholding from our land of living,
And forthwith found salvation in surrender.
Such as we were we gave ourselves outright
(The deed of gift was many gifts of war)
To the land vaguely realizing westward,
But still unstoried, artless, unenhanced,
Such as she was, such as she would become.

The third sentence is a little weakly and conventionally said; but the rest! And that *vaguely realizing westward!* The last three lines, both for tone and phrasing, are themselves realized with absolute finality, are good enough to survive all the repetitions that the generations of the future will give them.

We feel, here, that we understand why the lines are as good as they are; but sometimes there will be a sudden rise, an unlooked-for intensity and elevation of emotion, that have a conclusiveness and magnificence we are hardly able to explain. Frost ends a rather commonplace little poem about Time with a blaze of triumph, of calm and rapturous certainty, that is as transfiguring, almost, as the ending of "A Dialogue of Self and of Soul":

I could give all to Time except—except
What I myself have held. But why declare

> *The things forbidden that while the Customs slept*
> *I have crossed to Safety with? For I am There,*
> *And what I would not part with I have kept.*

A man finishes an axe-helve, and Frost says:

> *But now he brushed the shavings from his knee*
> *And stood the axe there on its horse's hoof,*
> *Erect, but not without its waves, as when*
> *The snake stood up for evil in the Garden . . .*

It would be hard to find words good enough for *this*. Surely anybody must feel, as he finishes reading these lines, the thrill of
authentic creation, the thrill of witnessing something that goes
back farther than Homer and goes forward farther than any
future we are able to imagine: here the thing in itself, and man's
naked wit, and Style—the elevation and composed forbearance
of the Grand Style, of the truly classical—coalesce in an instant
of grace.

Frost calls one poem "The Old Barn at the Bottom of the
Fogs," and starts out:

> *Where's this barn's house? It never had a house,*
> *Or joined with sheds in ring-around a dooryard.*
> *The hunter scuffling leaves goes by at dusk,*
> *The gun reversed that he went out with shouldered.*
> *The harvest moon and then the hunter's moon.*
> *Well, the moon after that came one at last*
> *To close this outpost barn and close the season.*
> *The fur-thing, muff-thing, rocking in and out*
> *Across the threshold in the twilight fled him . . .*

How can you resist a poet who can begin a poem like this—even if the poem later comes to nothing at all? Nor is it any easier to resist the man who says "To a Moth Seen in Winter," "with false hope seeking the love of kind," "making a labor of flight for one so airy":

> *Nor will you find love either nor love you.*
> *And what I pity in you is something human,*
> *The old incurable untimeliness,*
> *Only begetter of all things that are . . .*

What an already-prepared-for, already-familiar-seeming ring the lines have, the ring of that underlying style that great poets so often have in common beneath their own styles! I think that Dante would have read with nothing but admiration for its calm universal precision the wonderful "Acquainted with the Night," a poem in Dante's own form and with some of Dante's own qualities:

> *I have been one acquainted with the night.*
> *I have walked out in rain—and back in rain.*
> *I have outwalked the furthest city light.*
>
> *I have looked down the saddest city lane.*
> *I have passed by the watchman on his beat*
> *And dropped my eyes, unwilling to explain.*
>
> *I have stood still and stopped the sound of feet*
> *When far away an interrupted cry*
> *Came over houses from another street,*

But not to call me back or say goodbye;
And further still at an unearthly height,
One luminary clock against the sky

Proclaimed the time was neither wrong nor right.
I have been one acquainted with the night.

Is this a "classical" poem? If *it* isn't, what is? Yet doesn't the poem itself make the question seem ignominious, a question with a fatal lack of magnanimity, of true comprehension and concern? The things in themselves, the poem itself, abide neither our questions nor our categories; they are free. And our own freedom —the freedom to look and not to disregard, the freedom to side against oneself—is treated with delicate and tender imaginativeness in "Time Out":

It took that pause to make him realize
The mountain he was climbing had the slant
As of a book held up before his eyes
(And was a text albeit done in plant).
Dwarf-cornel, gold-thread, and maianthemum,
He followingly fingered as he read,
The flowers fading on the seed to come;
But the thing was the slope it gave his head:
The same for reading as it was for thought,
So different from the hard and level stare
Of enemies defied and battles fought.
It was the obstinately gentle air
That may be clamored at by cause and sect
But it will have its moment to reflect.

There is even more delicacy and tenderness and imagination in "Meeting and Passing," a backward-looking love-poem whose last two lines, by an understatement beyond statement, make tears of delight come into one's eyes—nothing else in English is so like one of those love-poems that, in 1913, Hardy wrote about a woman who had just died; and nothing else in English expresses better than that last couplet—which does not rhyme, but only repeats—the transfiguring, almost inexpressible reaching-out of the self to what has become closer and more personal than the self:

> *As I went down the hill along the wall*
> *There was a gate I had leaned at for the view*
> *And had just turned from when I first saw you*
> *As you came up the hill. We met. But all*
> *We did that day was mingle great and small*
> *Footprints in summer dust as if we drew*
> *The figure of our being less than two*
> *But more than one as yet. Your parasol*
>
> *Pointed the decimal off with one deep thrust.*
> *And all the time we talked you seemed to see*
> *Something down there to smile at in the dust*
> *(Oh, it was without prejudice to me!)*
> *Afterward I went past what you had passed*
> *Before we met and you what I had passed.*

And Frost (no poet has had even the range of his work more unforgiveably underestimated by the influential critics of our time) is able once or twice to give sexual love, passion itself, as breath-takingly conclusive an embodiment. Here I am not speaking of the sinister, condemning, tender "The Subverted Flower," a flawed but extraordinary poem that at once embodies and states in almost abstract form his knowledge about part of love; I mean the wonderful conclusion of "The Pauper Witch of Grafton," where the testy, acrid mockery of the old pauper, of the "noted witch" always plagued by an adulterous generation for a sign, turns into something very different as she remembers the man who first exposed and then married her:

> I guess he found he got more out of me
> By having me a witch. Or something happened
> To turn him round. He got to saying things
> To undo what he'd done and make it right,
> Like, "No, she ain't come back from kiting yet.
> Last night was one of her nights out. She's kiting.
> She thinks when the wind makes a night of it
> She might as well herself." But he liked best
> To let on he was plagued to death with me:
> If anyone had seen me coming home
> Over the ridgepole, 'stride of a broomstick,
> As often as he had in the tail of the night,
> He guessed they'd know what he had to put up with.
> Well, I showed Arthur Amy signs enough
> Off from the house as far as we could keep
> And from barn smells you can't wash out of ploughed ground
> With all the rain and snow of seven years;
> And I don't mean just skulls of Roger's Rangers
> On Moosilauke, but woman signs to man,

Only bewitched so I would last him longer.
Up where the trees grow short, the mosses tall,
I made him gather me wet snow berries
On slippery rocks beside a waterfall.
I made him do it for me in the dark.
And he liked everything I made him do.
I hope if he is where he sees me now
He's so far off he can't see what I've come to.
You can come down from everything to nothing.
All is, if I'd a-known when I was young
And full of it, that this would be the end,
It doesn't seem as if I'd had the courage
To make so free and kick up in folks' faces.
I might have, but it doesn't seem as if.

When I read the lines that begin *Up where the trees grow short,*
the mosses tall, and that end *And he liked everything I made him*
do (nobody but a good poet could have written the first line,
and nobody but a great one could have forced the reader to say
the last line as he is forced to say it), I sometimes murmur to
myself, in a perverse voice, that there is more sexuality there
than in several hothouses full of Dylan Thomas; and, of course,
there is love, there. And in what poem can one find more of its
distortion and frustration, its helpless derangement, than in
the marvellous "A Servant to Servants"? But here I come to
what makes the critic of Frost's poetry groan, and sadden, and
almost despair: several of his very best poems, the poems in
which he is most magnificent, most characteristic, most nearly
incomparable, are far too long to quote. If I could quote "Home

Burial," "The Witch of Coös," and "A Servant to Servants," Pharisee and Philistine alike would tiptoe off hand in hand, their shamed eyes starry; anyone who knows these poems well will consider the mere mention of them enough to justify any praise, any extravagance—and anybody who doesn't know them doesn't know some of the summits of our poetry, and is so much to be pitied that it would be foolish to blame him too. I don't know what to do about these poems, here: may I just make a bargain with the reader to regard them as quoted in this article?

I have used rather an odd tone about them because I feel so much frustration at not being able to quote and go over them, as I so often have done with friends and classes; they *do* crown Frost's work, are unique in the poetry of our century and perhaps in any poetry. Even such lesser poems of the sort as "The Fear" and "The Black Cottage" would be enough to make another poet respected; and it is discouraging, while mentioning Frost's poems about love, not to be able to quote "To Earthward" and "The Lovely Shall Be Choosers," two very beautiful and very unusual poems. And this reminds me that I have not even mentioned "Desert Places," a poem almost better, at the same game, than Stevens' beautiful "The Snowman." This is the best place to say once more that such an article as this is not relatively but absolutely inadequate to a body of poetry as great as Frost's, both in quality and in quantity—can be, at best, only a kind of breathless signboard. Almost all that Frost has touched, from the greatest to the smallest things, he has transfigured.

Frost is so characteristic and delightful in slight things, often,

that one feels a superstitious reluctance to dismiss them with
slight. The little "In a Disused Graveyard" is, plainly, the slight-
est and least pretentious of fancies; but the justest of fancies,
too—and how much there is underneath its last five lines, that
changes their shape almost as the least white of a wave-top is
changed by the green weight under it:

> *The living come with grassy tread*
> *To read the gravestones on the hill;*
> *The graveyard draws the living still,*
> *But never any more the dead.*
>
> *The verses in it say and say:*
> *"The ones who living come today*
> *To read the stones and go away*
> *Tomorrow dead will come to stay."*
>
> *So sure of death the marbles rhyme,*
> *Yet can't help marking all the time*
> *How no one dead will seem to come.*
> *What is it men are shrinking from?*
>
> *It would be easy to be clever*
> *And tell the stones: Men hate to die*
> *And have stopped dying now forever.*
> *I think they would believe the lie.*

Nothing could be slighter than these two lines called "The Span
of Life":

> *The old dog barks backward without getting up.*
> *I can remember when he was a pup.*

Yet the sigh we give after we've read them isn't a slight one: this is age in one couplet. And another couplet, one called "An Answer," I can hardly resist using as a sort of shibboleth or Stanford-Binet Test of the imagination: if you cannot make out the sea-change this strange little joke, this associational matrix, has undergone somewhere down in Frost's head, so that it has become worthy of Prospero himself, all nacreous with lyric, tender, amused acceptance and understanding and regret—if you can't feel any of this, you *are* a Convention of Sociologists. Here it is, "An Answer":

> *But Islands of the Blessèd, bless you son,*
> *I never came upon a blessèd one.*

Frost's account of a battle, in "Range-Finding," is an unprecedentedly slight one. This battle, before it killed any of the soldiers—and Frost does not go on to them—cut a flower beside a ground bird's nest, yet the bird kept flying in and out with food; and a butterfly, dispossessed of the flower, came back and flutteringly clung to it. Besides them there was

> *a wheel of thread*
> *And straining cables wet with silver dew.*
> *A sudden passing bullet shook it dry.*
> *The indwelling spider ran to greet the fly,*
> *But finding nothing, sullenly withdrew.*

That is all. An occasional lameness or tameness of statement mars the poem, gives it a queer rather attractive old-fashioned-ness, but does not destroy it. This is the minimal case, the final crystalline essence of Stendhal's treatment of Waterloo: a few fathoms down the sea is always calm, and a battle, among other things, at bottom is always this; the spider can ask with Fabrizio, "Was that it? Was I really at Waterloo?"

I mustn't go on quoting slight things forever, yet there are many more that I would like to quote—or that the reader might like to reread, or read: "An Empty Threat," "The Telephone," "Moon Compasses," "The Hill Wife," "Dust of Snow," "The Oven Bird," "Gathering Leaves" (that saddest, most-carefully-unspecified symbol for our memories), "For Once, Then, Something," "The Runaway," "In Hardwood Groves," "Beech," "The Ingenuities of Debt," "The Investment," the "Books" part of "A Fountain, a Bottle, a Donkey's Ear and Some Books" —these, and poems like "The Pasture" and "Stopping by Woods on a Snowy Evening," that many readers will not need to reread, but will simply repeat. (Frost is, often, as automatically memorable as any savage chronicle rhymed and metred for remembrance: I was floating in a quarry with my chin on a log when I first discovered that I knew "Provide Provide" by heart, and there are six or eight more that I know without ever having memorized them.) Here is a poem titled "Atmosphere," and subtitled "Inscription for a Garden Wall":

> *Winds blow the open grassy places bleak;*
> *But where this old wall burns a sunny cheek,*
> *They eddy over it too toppling weak*
> *To blow the earth or anything self-clear;*
> *Moisture and color and odor thicken here,*
> *The hours of daylight gather atmosphere.*

Now this is more than slight, it's nothing; I admit it; yet, admit it, isn't it a nothing that Marvell himself could have been proud of? And after reading it, can you understand how *any* critic could have patronizingly pigeonholed the man who wrote it? Frost writes a poem about a barn that is left over after its farmhouse has burnt down (of the house only the chimney is left, to stand "like a pistil after the petals go"); the poem is called "The Need of Being Versed in Country Things," and it ends:

> *The birds that came to it through the air*
> *At broken windows flew out and in,*
> *Their murmur more like the sigh we sigh*
> *From too much dwelling on what has been.*
>
> *Yet for them the lilac renewed its leaf,*
> *And the aged elm, though touched with fire;*
> *And the dry pump flung up an awkward arm;*
> *And the fence post carried a strand of wire.*
>
> *For them there was really nothing sad.*
> *But though they rejoiced in the nest they kept,*
> *One had to be versed in country things*
> *Not to believe the phoebes wept.*

But here I am not only left helpless to say whether this is slight or not, I don't even want to know: I am too sure of what I have even to want to say what it is, so that I will say if you ask me, as St. Augustine did about Time: "I know if you don't ask me."

I don't want to finish without saying how much *use* Frost's poems are to one, almost in the way that Hardy's are, when one has read them for many years—without saying how little they seem performances, no matter how brilliant or magical, how little things made primarily of words (or of ink and paper, either), and how much things made out of lives and the world that the lives inhabit. For how much this poetry *is* like the world, "the world wherein we find our happiness or not at all," "the world which was ere I was born, the world which lasts when I am dead," the world with its animals and plants and, most of all, its people: people working, thinking about things, falling in love, taking naps; in these poems men are not only the glory and jest and riddle of the world, but also the habit of the world, its strange ordinariness, its ordinary strangeness, and they too trudge down the ruts along which the planets move in their courses. Frost is that rare thing, a complete or representative poet, and not one of the brilliant partial poets who do justice, far more than justice, to a portion of reality, and leave the rest of things forlorn. When you know Frost's poems you know surprisingly well how the world seemed to one man, and what it was to seem that way: the great *Gestalt* that each of us makes from himself and all that isn't himself is very clear, very complicated, very contradictory in the poetry. The grimness and awfulness and untouchable sadness of things, both in the world and in the self, have justice done to them in the poems, but no more justice than is done to the tenderness and love and delight; and everything in between is represented somewhere too, some things willingly and often and other things only as much—in Marianne Moore's delicate phrase—"as one's natural reticence will allow." If some of the poems come out of a cynical commonsense that is only wisdom's backward shadow, others come out of wisdom itself—for it is, still, just possible for that most old-fashioned of old-fashioned things, wisdom, to maintain a marginal existence in our world. If we compare this wisdom with, say, that of the last of the Old Ones, Goethe, we are saddened and frightened at how much the poet's scope has narrowed, at how difficult and partial and idiosyncratic the application of his intelligence has become, at what terrible sacrifices he has had to make in order to avoid making others still more terrible. Yet how many poems, how many more lines, are immediately and supplely responsive with the unseparated unspecialized intelligence that is by now almost as natural to man—that being men have so laboriously created—as dreams and hunger and desire. To have the distance from the most awful and most nearly unbearable parts of the poems, to the most tender, subtle, and loving parts, a distance so great; to have this whole range of being treated with so much humor and sadness and composure, with such plain truth; to see that a man can still include, connect, and make humanly understandable or humanly ununderstandable so *much*—this is one of the freshest and oldest of joys, a joy strong enough to make us forget the limitations and excesses and baseness that these days seem unforgettable, a joy strong enough to make us say, with the Greek poet, that many things in this world are wonderful, but of all these the most wonderful is man.

The Age of Criticism

THERE is a subject that I cannot do justice to, but would like to treat even unjustly—a subject readers and novelists and poets often talk about, but almost never write about: our age of criticism. Perhaps I ought only to talk or, at most, write a verse satire about it; one can say anything in verse and no one will mind. I wish that you would treat what I am going to write as if it were verse or talk, a conversation-with-no-one about our age of criticism. It is only a complaint, perhaps more false than true—partial, and full of exaggerations and general impressions; but it is a complaint that people do make, and may at least relieve their feelings and mine. And I will try to spare other people's by using no names at all.

The common reader does not know that it is an age of criticism, and for him it is not. He reads (seldomer and seldomer now) historical novels, the memoirs of generals, whatever is successful; good books, sometimes—good books too are successful. He cannot tell the book editor of the Chicago *Tribune* from

Samuel Johnson, and is neither helped nor hindered by criticism
—to him a critic is a best-seller list, only less so. Such a reader
lives in a pleasant, anarchic, oblivious world, a world as democratic, almost, as the warm dark depths below, where nobody
reads anything but newspapers and drugstore-books and comic-
books and the *Reader's Digest* at the dentist's. This common
reader knows what he likes, but is uncomfortable when other
people do not read it or do not like it—for what people read and
like is good: that is what *good* means.

On the slopes above (as a fabulist might put it) live many
races of animals: the most numerous are the members of Book
Clubs and the dwellers in the Land of Book Reviews. These find
out from their leaders weekly, monthly, what they ought to read,
what they ought to like; and since, thank goodness, that is almost always what they would have read and liked anyway,
without the help of the reviewers, they all live in unity and
amity. It is the country of King Log, the fabulist would say:
thousands of logs lie booming on the hillside, while their subjects
croak around them; if you shut your eyes it is hard to tell who
reads, who writes, and who reviews . . . Nearby one finds
readers of scholarly journals, readers of magazines of experiment,
readers of magazines of verse. But highest of all, in crevices of the
naked rock, cowering beneath the keen bills of the industrious
storks, dwell our most conscious and, perhaps, most troubled
readers; and for these—cultivated or academic folk, intellectuals,
"serious readers," the leaven of our queer half-risen loaf—this is
truly an age of criticism. It is about them and their Stork-Kings
that I am going to talk for the rest of this article.

Four times a year (six if they read *Partisan Review*) these people read or try to read or wish that they had read large magazines called literary quarterlies. Each of these contains several poems and a piece of fiction—sometimes two pieces; the rest is criticism.

The rest is criticism. The words have a dull uneasy sound; they lie on the spirit with a heavy weight. There has never been an age in which so much good criticism has been written—or so *much* bad; and both of them have become, among "serious readers," astonishingly or appallingly influential. I am talking as a reader of the criticism of the last few years to other readers of it, and am assuming that we recognize its merits and services, which are great; I myself can and do read the magazines that I have been talking about, and they seem to me the best magazines that we have—the magazines which enjoy attacking them are almost ludicrously inferior to them. But, I think, they print far too much criticism, and far too much of the criticism that they print is of a kind that is more attractive to critics and to lovers of criticism than it is to poets and fiction-writers and to lovers of poetry and fiction. Criticism *does* exist, doesn't it, for the sake of the plays and stories and poems it criticizes? Much of this criticism does not; much of it gives a false idea of the nature and use of criticism, a false idea of the variety and importance of critics.

Some of this criticism is as good as anyone could wish: several of the best critics alive print most of their work in such magazines as these. Some more of this criticism is intelligent and useful—it sounds as if it had been written by a reader for readers, by a human being for human beings. But a great deal of this criticism might just as well have been written by a syndicate of encyclopedias for an audience of International Business Machines. It is not only bad or mediocre, it is *dull;* it is, often, an astonishingly graceless, joyless, humorless, long-winded, niggling, blinkered, methodical, self-important, cliché-ridden, prestige-obsessed, almost-autonomous criticism. Who *can* believe that either readers or writers are helped by most of the great leaden articles on Great or currently fashionable writers—always the same fifteen or twenty, if the critic can manage it—which encounter us as regularly as the equinoxes and the solstices? I have heard intelligent and cultivated people complain more times than I can remember, "I can hardly *read* the quarterlies any more"; and I once heard Elizabeth Bishop say, "After I go through one of the literary quarterlies I don't feel like reading a poem for a week, much less like writing one." Many other people have felt so; and for weeks or months or years afterwards they have neither read poems nor written them, but have criticized. For—one begins to see—an age of criticism is not an age of writing, nor an age of reading: it is an age of criticism. People still read, still write—and well; but for many of them it is the act of criticism which has become the representative or Archetypal act of the intellectual.

Critics may still be rather negligible figures in comparison to the composers and painters they write about; but when they write about writers, what a difference! A novelist, a friend of mine, one year went to a Writers' Conference; all the other teachers were critics, and each teacher had to give a formal public lecture. My friend went to the critics' lectures, but the critics didn't go to his; he wasn't surprised; as he said, "You could tell they knew I wasn't really literary like them." Recently

I went to a meeting at which a number of critics discussed what Wordsworth had said about writing poetry. It was interesting to me to see how consciously or unconsciously patronizing they were to—poor Wordsworth, I almost wrote. They could see what he had meant, confused as he was, layman that he was; and because he had been, they supposed they must admit, a great poet, it did give what he had to say a wonderful documentary interest, like Nelson's remarks at Trafalgar. But the critics could not help being conscious of the difference between themselves, and Wordsworth, and my friend: *they* knew how poems and novels are put together, and Wordsworth and my friend didn't, but had just put them together. In the same way, if a pig wandered up to you during a bacon-judging contest, you would say impatiently, "Go away, pig! What do you know about bacon?"

It is no wonder that, in some of the places where critics are most concentrated, and their influence most overpowering, people write less and less. (By *write* I mean *write stories, poems, or plays.*) Some boys at a large and quite literary college I visited were telling me how much trouble they have getting poems and stories for the college's magazine. "There are only four or five we can depend on much," the editor said sadly; "everybody else that's any good writes criticism." I suppose I should have said to him, "Make the magazine criticism"; after all, isn't that the way you run a literary magazine?—but I hadn't the heart to.

These days, when an ambitious young intellectual finishes college, he buys himself a new typewriter, rents himself a room, and settles down to write . . . book reviews, long critical articles, explications. "As for living, our servants can do that for us," said Villiers de l'Isle Adam; and in the long run this gets said not only of living but also of writing stories and poems, which is almost as difficult and helpless and risky as living. Why stick one's neck out so far for so little? It is hard to write even a competent naturalistic story, and when you have written it what happens?—someone calls it a competent naturalistic story. Write another "Horatian Ode," and you will be praised as "one of the finest of our minor poets." No, as anyone can see, it is hardly worthwhile being a writer unless you can be a great one; better not sell your soul to the Muse till she has shown you the critical articles of 2100. Unless you are one of a dozen or so writers you will have a life like Trigorin's; he said that they would put on his tombstone that he had been a fine writer, *but not so good as Turgenev*—and sure enough, if you go and look on his tombstone that is what is there. Our Trigorins can hardly fail to see that, in serious critical circles, the very recognition of their merit dismisses it and them; there is written on their hearts in little red letters, "It's only me." I never remember hearing *anybody* say of a critic, "He's all right, but he's no Saint-Beuve"; but substitute *Dante* or some such O. K. name for *Saint-Beuve*, and there are very few writers about whom the statement hasn't been made. When the first book of one of the best of living poets was published, one of the best of living critics said about it only that it was "grating," and lacked the sweetness of the *Divine Comedy*. So it did; the poet might have replied with the same truth that his critic lacked Matthew Arnold's yellow kid gloves.

Critics can easily infect their readers (though usually less by precept than example) with the contempt or fretful tolerance which they feel for "minor" works of art. If you work away, with sober, methodical, and industrious complication, at the master-pieces of a few great or fashionable writers, you after a while begin to identify yourself with these men; your manner takes on the authority your subject matter has unwittingly delegated to you, and when—returned from the peaks you have spent your life among, picking a reluctant way over those Parnassian or Castalian foothills along whose slopes herdboys sit playing combs—you are required to judge the competitions of such artists, you do so with a certain reluctance. Everybody has observed this in scholars, who feel that live authors, as such, are self-evidently inferior to dead ones; though a broadminded scholar will look like an X-ray machine at such a writer as Thomas Mann, and feel, relenting: "He's as good as dead." This sort of thing helps to make serious criticism as attractive as it is to critics: they live among the great, and some of the greatness comes off on them. No wonder poor poets become poor critics, and count themselves blest in their bargain; no wonder young intellectuals become critics before, and not after, they have failed as artists. And sometimes—who knows?—they might not have failed; besides, to have failed as an artist may be a respectable and valuable thing.

Some of us write less; all of us, almost, read less—the child at his television set, the critic or novelist in the viewplate of the set, grayly answering questions on topics of general interest. Children have fewer and fewer empty hours, and the eight-year-old is discouraged from filling them with the books written for his brother of ten; nor is anyone at his school surprised when he does not read very much or very well—it is only "born readers" who do that.

But if we read less and less—by *we*, this time, I mean the cultivated minority—a greater and greater proportion of what we read is criticism. Many a man last read *Moby Dick* in the eleventh grade, *The Brothers Karamazov* in his freshman year in college; but think of all the articles about them he's read since! It is no use to tell such a reader, "Go read *Moby Dick*"; he would only answer, "I've read it," and start out on the latest book about Melville. And imagine how he would look at you if you told him to read, say, *Kim*. In such a case, whether he has or hasn't read it doesn't matter: he knows that he doesn't need to. It is criticism, after all, which protects us from the bad or unimportant books that we would otherwise have to read; and during the time we have saved we can read more of the criticism which protects us. I imagine, in gray hours, a generation which will have read a few masterpieces, a few thousand criticisms of these, and almost nothing else but—as the generation will say apologetically—"trash." It is an Alexandrian notion, but in many ways we *are* Alexandrian; and we do not grow less so with the years. I was told recently two awful and delightful instances of the specialization, the dividing into categories, of people's unlucky lives. A student at Harvard, taking his final examinations for a Ph.D. in English, was asked to make a short criticism of some contemporary book he had read and liked. This was the first question to give him any trouble—he had been particularly good on Middle English; he said after a while, "I don't believe I've read any contemporary books—at least not since I've been in college." Another student, taking *his* final examinations at Princeton, was asked to summarize Tennyson's "Ulysses." He did. "How does this treatment of Ulysses compare with that in the *Divine Comedy?*" someone asked. The student said that he didn't know, he hadn't read the *Divine Comedy*. "How does Tennyson's Ulysses compare with the one in the *Odyssey?*" someone else asked. The student said that he didn't know, he hadn't read the *Odyssey*. Both students were scolded and passed, and their professors came home to tell me the stories.

These men were indeed specialists in English. And yet, reader, aren't many intellectuals almost as great specialists in Important —that is to say, currently fashionable—books? Many of the intellectuals whom one hears discussing books certainly do not seem to have read widely or enthusiastically. Talking with an excellent critic and historian of ideas—a professor, too, *à la* Matthew Arnold—I asked him whether his students read much. He said, "My students! I can't get my colleagues to read anything!" Of course he was exaggerating; I felt that he was exaggerating very much; but it troubled me to remember the conversation at the literary parties at which he and I had occasionally met. Here people talked about few books, perhaps, but the books they talked about were the same: it was like the Middle Ages. And—this was like the Middle Ages too—they seemed more interested in the books' commentators than in the books; though when the books were Great, this was not always so. If you talked about the writings of some minor American novelist or short-story writer or poet—by *minor*, here, I mean anybody but the immediately fashionable six or eight—your hearer's eyes began to tap their feet almost before you had finished a sentence. (I have to admit that if you talked about such writers' unfortunate lives, and not their unfortunate writings, this didn't happen: lives, however minor, keep their primitive appeal.) But if you talked about what the ten-thousandth best critic in the country had just written, in the last magazine, about the next-worse critic's analysis of *The Ambassadors*, their eyes shone, they did not even interrupt you. There are few things more interesting to people of this sort than what a bad critic says of a bad criticism of a fashionable writer; what a good critic says of good criticism of him is equally interesting, if it is equally difficult, complicated, or novel.

If, at such parties, you wanted to talk about *Ulysses* or *The Castle* or *The Brothers Karamazov* or *The Great Gatsby* or Graham Greene's last novel—Important books—you were at the right place. (Though you weren't so well off if you wanted to talk about *Remembrance of Things Past*. Important, but too long.) But if you wanted to talk about Turgenev's novelettes, or *The House of the Dead*, or *Lavengro*, or *Life on the Mississippi*, or *The Old Wives' Tale*, or *The Golovlyov Family*, or Cunningham-Grahame's stories, or Saint-Simon's memoirs, or *Lost Illusions*, or *The Beggar's Opera*, or *Eugen Onegin*, or *Little Dorrit*, or the *Burnt Njal Saga*, or *Persuasion*, or *The Inspector-General*, or *Oblomov*, or *Peer Gynt*, or *Far from the Madding Crowd*, or *Out of Africa*, or the *Parallel Lives*, or *A Dreary Story*, or *Debits and Credits*, or *Arabia Deserta*, or *Elective Affinities*, or *Schweik*, or—or any of a thousand good or interesting but Unimportant books, you couldn't expect a very ready knowledge or sympathy from most of the readers there. They had looked at the big sights, the current sights, hard, with guides and glasses; and those walks in the

country, over unfrequented or thrice-familiar territory, all alone
—those walks from which most of the joy and good of reading
come—were walks that they hadn't gone on very often. And unless they were poets or poetry-critics, or of the minority that
still is fond of poems, they weren't likely to know much poetry.
Nothing would surprise the readers of another age more than the
fact that to most of us literature is primarily fiction. It still surprises visitors from another culture: a Colombian student of
mine, marvelling at it, said, "In my country business men, quite
a good many of them, write poetry; and when the maid cleans my
room, she often picks up one of my poetry books and reads in it."
When he said this I remembered that the critic and historian of
ideas I spoke of had said to me, in a tone he would not have used
for prose: "Now about *Paterson*—what do you think of it? Is it
really much good?" I amused myself by trying to imagine Dr.
Johnson asking Christopher Smart this about Gray's *Elegy*.

Many of the critics one reads or meets make an odd impression
about reading, one that might be given this exaggerated em-
blematic form: "Good Lord, you don't think I *like* to read, do
you? Reading is serious business, not something you fool around
with in your spare time." Such critics read, pencil in hand, the
books they have to read for an article, have to read for basic
literary conversation—although most of these last, they are glad
to think, they got through long ago. Readers, real readers, are almost as wild a species as writers; most critics are so domesticated
as to seem institutions—as they stand there between reader and
writer, so different from either, they remind one of the Wall
standing between Pyramus and Thisbe. And some of *their* constant readers are so serious, responsible, and timid about reading

a great work that they start out on it with a white hunter, native bearers, and a $10,000 policy they bought from the insurance-machine at the airport. The critics got back, but who knows whether they will be able to?

To the question "Have you read *Gerontion*?"—or some other poem that may seem difficult to people—I've several times heard people reply: "Well, not really—I've *read* it, but I've never read a thorough analysis of it, or really gone through it systematically." And one critic will say of another critic's analysis of a book like *Moby Dick:* "Mr. Something has given us the first thorough [or *systematic*] reading of *Moby Dick* that we have had." After people had leafed through it for so long, it's at last been read! Yet, often, how plain and actual the poem or story itself seems, compared to those shifting and contradictory and all-too-systematic "readings" that veil it as clouds veil the rocks of a mountain. Luckily, we can always seek refuge from the analyses in the poem itself—*if we like poems better than we like analyses*. But poems, stories, new-made works of art, are coming to seem rather less congenial and important than they once did, both to literary and not-so-literary readers. So far as the last are concerned, look at the lists of best-sellers, the contents of popular magazines—notice how cheerful and beefy *Time* is when it's reviewing a biography, how grumpy and demanding it gets as soon as it's reviewing a serious novel. And look at the literary quarterlies, listen to the conversation of literary people: how much of it is criticism of criticism, talk about talk about books!

People realize that almost all fiction or poetry is bad or mediocre—it's the nature of things. Almost all criticism is bad or mediocre too, but it's harder for people to tell; and even commonplace criticism can seem interesting or important simply because of its subject matter. An English statesman said that he liked the Order of the Garter because there was *no damned merit involved;* there is no damned inspiration involved in the writing of criticism, generally, and that is what the literary magazines like about it—there is an inexhausti ble, unexceptionable, indistinguishable supply. They are not interested in being wildcat drillers for oil, but had rather have a hydro-electric plant at Niagara Falls. This was always the policy of the *Criterion*, their immediate ancestor: it gave a bare token representation to the literature of the '20's and '30's, and used up its space on criticism, much of it by J. Middleton Murry, John Gould Fletcher, and other Faithful Contributors.

A friend said to me one day, after he had opened his mail: "Whenever I have a story published, I get two or three letters asking me to write reviews." It isn't any different with poets. A young critic—one who makes his living by teaching, as most serious young critics do—could say in practical justification of his work: "If you're a critic the magazines *want* you to write for them, they *ask* you to write for them—there's all that space just waiting to be filled with big articles, long reviews. Look at this quarterly: 2½ pages of poems, 11 of a story, 134 of criticism. My job depends on my getting things printed. What chance have *I* got to get in those 13½ pages? Me for the 134!" So he might speak. But the chances are that it has never even occurred to the young critic to write a story or a poem. New critic is but old scholar writ large, as a general thing: the same gifts which used to go into proving that the Wife of Bath was really an aunt of Chaucer's named Alys Persë now go into proving that all of

Henry James's work is really a Swedenborgian allegory. Criticism will soon have reached the state of scholarship, and the most obviously absurd theory—if it is maintained intensively, exhaustively, and professionally—will do the theorist no harm in the eyes of his colleagues.

But one must remember (or remain a child where criticism is concerned) that a great deal of the best and most sensible criticism of any age *is necessarily absurd.* Hundreds of examples will occur to anybody: Goethe and Schiller thought so little of Hölderlin that after a while they wouldn't even answer his letters. "Ah, but *we* wouldn't have been so foolish as Goethe and Schiller," we always feel; "you won't catch *us* making that mistake." And you don't: we love Hölderlin. But some duckling we have never spared a smile for is *our* Hölderlin, and half the swans we spent our Sundays feeding bread-crumbs to will turn out to have been Southeys. And just as we will have been wrong about such people, so all of our critics will have been wrong: it's their *métier,* isn't it?—it always has been. It is easy to nod to all this as a truism, but it is hard to feel it as a truth. To feel it is to be fortified in the independence and humility that we as readers ought to have.

Once critics wrote as best they could, like anybody else—they knew no better; but today many of them have a language and style as institutionalized as those of sociologists. They have managed to develop this style in fifteen or twenty years—one finds only its crude beginnings in the *Hound and Horn* and the *Dial;* the critics of those days may have sounded superior and difficult to the readers of those days, but to us, now, they seem endearingly amateurish and human and informal, so that one looks at some essay and thinks, smiling, "That was certainly the *Paul et Virginie* stage of Kenneth Burke." Who had perfected, then, that strange sort of Law French which the critic now can set up like a Chinese Wall between himself and the lay (i.e., boreable) reader? The first generation wrote distinguishably well; the second writes indistinguishably ill; who knows how the third will write? Academic or scholarly writing has some bad qualities, and the writing of Superior Intellectuals has others: the style that I am describing almost combines the two. It is a style, a tone, that is hard to picture: if the two bears that ate the forty-two little children who said to Elisha, "Go up, thou baldhead"—if they, after getting their Ph.D.'s from the University of Göttingen, had retired to Atta Troll's Castle and written a book called *A Prolegomena to Every Future Criticism of Finnegans Wake*, they might have written so.

This style partly is a result of the difficult or once-difficult position of such critics (and of such intellectuals in general) in both our universities and our general literary culture. Sociologists went in for jargon, psychologists for graphs and statistics, mostly because they knew that physicists and chemists and biologists did not think sociology and psychology sciences; English professors did the same thing for the same reason; and the critics in the universities probably felt a similar need to show the scholars who looked down on them that criticism is just as difficult and just as much of a science as "English." But the literary quarterlies are also "little magazines," revolutionary organs of an oppressed or neglected class; their contributors, by using a style which insists upon their superiority to the society that disregards them, both protect themselves and punish their society.

84

One can understand why so many critics find it necessary to worry and weary their readers to death, in the most impressive way possible; if they themselves understood, they might no longer find it necessary. Or so one thinks—but one is naive to think it: this style or tone of theirs is a spiritual necessity, and how can they give it up without finding something to put in its place? What began in need has been kept and elaborated in love. And I don't want them put out of their misery, I am only crying to them out of mine. May one of them say to the others, soon: "Brothers, *do* we want to sound like the *Publications of the Modern Language Association*, only worse? If we don't set things straight for ourselves, others will set them straight for us—or worse still, others won't, and things will go on as they are going on until one day even you and I won't be able to read each other, for sheer boredom."

Of course I do not mean that critics should all go out and try to have Styles, or that we should judge them by the way they write —though an absolutely bad writer is at least relatively incapable of distinguishing between good and bad in the writing that he criticizes. It is his reading that we judge a critic by, not his writing. The most impressive thing about the good critic is the fact that he *does* respond to the true nature and qualities of a work of art—not always, but often. But to be impressed by this you must be able to see these qualities when they are pointed out to you: that is, you have to be under favorable circumstances almost as good a reader as the critic is under less favorable ones. Similarly, the most impressive thing about the bad critic is his methodical and oblivious contempt for unfashionable master-pieces, his methodical and superstitious veneration for fashionable masterpieces and their reflections; but to be properly impressed with this you must have responded to the works themselves, and not to their reputations. There is a Critical Dilemma which might be put in this form: To be able to tell which critics are reliable guides to literature, you must know enough about literature not to need guides. (This is a less-than-half-truth, but a neglected one.) What we need, it might seem, is somebody who can tell us not which are the good and bad writers, but which are the good and bad critics; and half the critics I know are also trying to supply this need. In literature it is not that we have a labyrinth without a clue; the clues themselves have become a worse labyrinth, a perfect Navy Yard of great coiling hawsers which we are supposed to pay out behind us on our way into the darkness of—oh, "To His Coy Mistress," or whatever it is we're reading.

It is easier for the ordinary reader to judge among poems or stories or plays than it is for him to judge among pieces of criticism. Many bad or commonplace works of art never even succeed in getting him to notice them, and there *are* masterpieces which can shake even the Fat Boy awake. Good critics necessarily disagree with some of the reader's dearest convictions—unless he is a Reader among readers—and they are likely to seem offensive in doing so. But the bad or commonplace critic can learn very easily (as easily as a preacher or politician, almost) which are the right people to look down on or up to, and what are the right things to write for any occasion, the things his readers will admire and agree with almost before he has written them. And he can write in an impressive and authoritative way; can use a definitive tone, big words, great weighty sentences, Clinching

References—the plagues of Egypt couldn't equal all the references to Freud and Jung and Marx and myths and existentialism and neo-Calvinism and Aristotle and St. Thomas that you'll sometimes see in one commonplace article. ("If he knows all these things how can he be wrong about a little thing like a poem?" the reader may well feel.) It is perpetually tempting to the critic to make his style and method so imposing to everyone that nobody will notice or care when he is wrong. And if the critic is detailedly and solemnly enthusiastic about the great, and rather silent and condescending about the small, how *can* he go very badly wrong? make a complete fool of himself? But taking the chance of making a complete fool of himself—and, sometimes, doing so—is the first demand that is made upon any real critic: he *must* stick his neck out just as the artist does, if he is to be of any real use to art.

The essential merit of a critic, then, is one that it is hard for many of his readers to see. Critics have a wonderfully imposing look, but this is only because they are in a certain sense impostors: the judges' black gowns, their positions and degrees and qualifications, their professional accomplishments, methods, styles, distinctions—all this institutional magnificence hides from us the naked human beings who do the judging, the fallible creatures who are what the accidents of birth and life have left them. If, as someone says, we ought not to forget that a masterpiece is something written by a man sitting alone in a room before a sheet of paper, we ought not to forget that a piece of criticism is produced in the same way: we have no substitute for these poor solitary human souls who do the writing, the criticizing and, also, the reading of poems and stories and novels. (I did recently meet a Scandinavian social scientist who said that after "an extension of the statistical methods of public opinion polls," this would no longer be true.) It is easy for readers and critics to forget this: "Extraordinary advances in critical method," writes an innocent anthologist, "make the inspection of a poem today by a first-rate critic as close and careful as a chemical analysis." As close and as careful, perhaps, but more delightfully unpredictable: for these are chemists who, half the time, after the long weeks of analysis are over, can't even agree whether what they were analyzing was bread or beer. An *Encyclopedia of Pseudo-Sciences* might define critical method as *the systematic (q.v.) application of foreign substances to literature; any series of devices by which critics may treat different works of art as much alike as possible.* It is true that a critical method can help us neither to read nor to judge; still, it is sometimes useful in pointing out to the reader a few gross discrete reasons for thinking a good poem good—and it is invaluable, almost indispensable, in convincing a reader that a good poem is bad, or a bad one good. (The best critic who ever lived could not *prove* that the *Iliad* is better than *Trees;* the critic can only state his belief persuasively, and hope that the reader of the poem will agree—but *persuasively* covers everything from a sneer to statistics.)

We do not become good critics by reading criticism and, secondarily, the "data" or "raw material" of criticism: that is, poems and stories. We become good critics by reading poems and stories and by living; it is reading criticism which is secondary—if it often helps us a great deal, it often hinders us more: even a good critic or reader has a hard time recovering from the taste of the age which has produced him. Many bad critics are bad, I think, because they have spent their life in card-indexes; or if they have not, no one can tell. If works of art were about card-indexes the critic could prepare for them in this way, but as it is he cannot. An interesting book about recent criticism was called *The Armed Vision;* the title and a few of the comments on the qualities of the ideal modern critic suggested that he would rather resemble one of those robots you meet in science-fiction stories, with a microscope for one eye, a telescope for the other, and the mechanical brain at Harvard for a heart.

Everybody understands that poems and stories are written by memory and desire, love and hatred, daydreams and nightmares—by a being, not a brain. But they are read just so, judged just so; and some great lack in human qualities is as fatal to the critic as it is to the novelist. Someone asked Eliot about critical method, and he replied: "The only method is to be very intelligent." And this is of course only a beginning: there have been many very intelligent people, but few good critics—far fewer than there have been good artists, as any history of the arts will tell you. "Principles" or "standards" of excellence are either specifically harmful or generally useless; the critic has nothing to go by except his experience as a human being and a reader, and is the personification of empiricism. A Greek geometer said that there is no royal road to geometry—there is no royal, or systematic, or impersonal, or rational, or safe, or sure road to criticism. Most people understand that a poet is a good poet because he does well some of the time; this is true of critics—if we are critics we can see this right away for everybody except ourselves, and everybody except ourselves can see it right away about *us.* But many critics have the bearing of people who are right all the time, and most of us like this: it makes them look more like our fathers.

Real criticism demands of human beings an almost inhuman disinterestedness, one which they adopt with reluctance and maintain with difficulty: the real critic must speak ill of friends and well of enemies, ill of agreeable bad works and well of less agreeable good ones; must admire writers whom his readers will snicker at him for admiring, and dislike writers whom it will place him among barbarians to dislike. For it is the opinion he offers with trepidation, thinking: "Nobody will believe it, and I hardly see how it can be so; but it seems so to me"—it is this opinion that may be all the next age will value him for; though in all probability it will value him for nothing—critics had better make the best of their own age, for few of them ever survive to the next. Criticism demands of the critic a terrible nakedness: a real critic has no one but himself to depend on. He can never forget that all he has to go by, finally, is his own response, the self that makes and is made up of such responses—and yet he must regard that self as no more than the instrument through which the work of art is seen, so that the work of art will seem everything to him and his own self nothing: the good critic has, as Eliot says, a great "sense of fact." Real critics do some of the time see what is there, even when—especially when—it is not what they want to be there. The critic must in this sense get away from his self-as-self; and he must as much as he can, for as long as he can, train and expose and widen this self, get rid of all that he can see as merely self—prejudices and disabilities and predilections—without ever losing the personal truth of judgment that his criticism springs from. (In the end the critic disappears, like the rest of us, in the quicksand of his own convictions.) Real criticism demands not only unusual human qualities but an unusual combination and application of these: it is no wonder that even real critics are just critics, most of the time. So much of our society is based, necessarily, on lies, equivocations, glossings-over; a real critic, about a part of this society, tries to tell only the truth. When it is a pleasant truth—and it often is—reader and writer and critic are a joy to one another; but when the critic comes to the reader's house and tells him, causelessly and senselessly and heartlessly, that the book he is married to isn't everything she should be—ah, then it's a different affair!

But I have been talking of a "real critic" who would have a very short half-life, one who may never have been on sea or land; let me talk instead about good ordinary ones—viable ones, as a Modern Critic would say. What *is* a critic, anyway? So far as I can see, he is an extremely good reader—one who has learned to show to others what he saw in what he read. He is always many other things too, but these belong to his accident, not his essence. Of course, it is often the accident and not the essence that we read the critic for: pieces of criticism are frequently, though not necessarily, works of art of an odd anomalous kind, and we can sympathize with someone when he says lovingly about a critic, as Empson says about I. A. Richards, that we get more from *him* when he's wrong than we do from other people when they're right. I myself have sometimes felt this way about Empson; and the reader surely has his favorites too, writers to whom he goes for style and wit and sermons, informal essays, aesthetics, purple passages, confessions, aphorisms, wisdom—a thousand things. (One occasionally encounters intellectual couples for whom some critic has taken the place of the minister they no longer have.) Critics—I admit it very willingly—are often useful and wonderful and a joy to have around the house; *but* they're the bane of our age, because our age so fantastically overestimates their importance and so willingly forsakes the works they are writing about for them. We are brought into the world by specialists, borne out of it by specialists: more and more people think of the critic as an indispensable middle man between writer and reader, and would no more read a book alone, if they could help it, than have a baby alone. How many of us seem to think that the poem or story is in some sense "data" or "raw material" which the critic cooks up into understanding, so that we say, "I'd just never *read* 'We Are Seven' till I got So-and-So's analysis of it for Christmas!" But the work of art is as done as it will ever get, and all the critics in the world can't make its crust a bit browner; they may help *us*, the indigent readers, but they haven't done a thing to it. Around the throne of God, where all the angels read perfectly, there are no critics—there is no need for them.

Critics exist simply to help us with works of art—isn't that true? Once, talking to a young critic, I said as a self-evident thing, "Of course, criticism's necessarily secondary to the works of art it's about." He looked at me as if I had kicked him, and said: "Oh, that's not *so!*" (I had kicked him, I realized.) And recently I heard a good critic, objecting to most of the criticism in the quarterlies, say what *real* criticism did: what it did, as he put it, was almost exactly what people usually say that religion, love, and great works of art do. Criticism, which began by humbly and anomalously existing for the work of art, and was in part a mere by-product of philosophy and rhetoric, has by now become, for a good many people, almost what the work of art exists for: the animals come up to Adam and Eve and are named—the end crowns the work.

There is an atmosphere or environment, at some of the higher levels of our literary culture, in which many people find it almost impossible not to write criticism and almost impossible to write anything else, if they pay much attention to the critics. For these fond mothers not only want the artist to be good, they want him to be great; and not simply great, but great in just the way he should be: they want him to be exactly the same as, only somehow entirely different from, the *Divine Comedy*. If the reader says, "It's always been that way," I'll answer, "Of course, of course. But critics are so much better armed than they used to be in the old days: they've got tanks and flame-throwers now, and it's harder to see past them to the work of art—in fact, magnificent creatures that they are, it's hard to *want* to see past them. Can't you imagine an age in which critics are like paleontologists, an age in which the last bone that the youngest critic has wired together is already hundreds of years old? Scholars are like that now. And critics are already like conductors, and give you *their* 'Lear,' *their* 'Confidence Man,' *their* 'Turn of the Screw.' It's beginning to frighten me a little; do we really *want* it to be an Age of Criticism?"

Ben Jonson called one of his poems "A Fit of Rhyme against Rhyme," and perhaps I should have called this article "A Fit of Criticism against Criticism." But of course I'm complaining not just about criticism and the literary quarterlies, but about the age; and that's only fair—what is an age but something to complain about? But if the age, the higher literary levels of it, doesn't wish to be an age of criticism, and an increasingly Alexandrian one at that, it needs to care more for stories and novels and poems and plays, and less for criticism; it needs to read more widely, more independently, and more joyfully; and it needs to say to its critics: "Write so as to be of some use to a reader—a reader, that is, of poems and stories, not of criticism. Vary a little, vary a little! Admit what you can't conceal, that criticism is no more than (and no less than) the helpful remarks and the thoughtful and disinterested judgment of a reader, a loving and experienced and able reader, but only a reader. And remember that works of art are never data, raw material, the crude facts that you critics explain or explain away. Remember that you can never be more than the staircase to the monument, the guide to the gallery, the telescope through which the children see the stars. At your best you make people see what they might never have seen without you; but they must always forget you in what they see."

Since I have complained of the style and method of much of the criticism that we read, I ought to say now that I know my own are wrong for this article. An article like this ought, surely, to avoid satire; it ought to be documented and persuasive and sympathetic, much in sorrow and hardly at all in anger—the reader should not be able to feel the wound for the balm. And yet a suitable article might not do any more good than this sort: people have immediate and irresistible reasons for what they do, and cannot be much swayed by helpful or vexing suggestions from bystanders. But if because of an article like this, or because of the better one that I hope someone else will write, a few people read a story instead of a criticism, write a poem instead of a review, pay no attention to what the most systematic and definitive critic says against some work of art they love—if that happens, the articles will have been worth writing.

John Ransom's Poetry

THE SUBJECT-MATTER of Ransom's poetry is beautifully varied: the poems are about everything from Armageddon to a dead hen. All their subjects are linked, on the surface, by Ransom's persistent attitude, tone, and rhetoric; at bottom they are joined, passively, by being parts of one world—joined, actively, by fighting on one side or the other in the war that is going on in that world. On one side are Church and State, Authority, the Business World, the Practical World, men of action, men of affairs, generals and moralists and applied mathematicians and philosophers you set your watch by—efficient followers of abstraction and ideals, men who have learned that when you know how to use something you know it. There is a good deal of rather mocking but quite ungrudging credit—if little fondness—given to this side of things, the motor or effector system which, after all, does run the world along its "metalled ways" of appetency (our version of Tennyson's "ringing grooves of change"). But Ransom's affection goes out to that other army, defeated every day and victorious every night, of so-lightly-armed, so-easily-vanquished skirmishers, in their rags and tags and trailing clouds, who run around and around the iron hoplites pelting them with gravel and rosemary, getting killed miserably, and—half the time, in the pure pleasure or pain of being—forgetting even that they are fighting, and wandering off into the flowers at the edge of the terrible field. Here are the "vessels fit for storm and sport," not yet converted into "miserly merchant hulls"—the grandfather dancing with his fierce grandsons, in warpaint and feathers, round a bonfire in the back yard, having "performed ignominies unreckoned/ Between the first brief childhood and the second," but now "more honorable . . . in danger and in joy." In these ranks are children and the old, women—innocent girls or terrible beauties or protecting housewives, all above or below or at the side of the Real World—lovers, dreams, nature, animals, tradition, nursery rhymes, fairy tales, everything that is at first or at last "content to feel/ What others understand." Sometimes the poems are—as Empson might say—a queer mixture of pastoral and childcult. Although the shepherds are aging and the children dead, half of them, and the fox-hunters not making much headway against the overweening Platonism of the International Business Machine Company, it is all magical: disenchantment and enchantment are so prettily and inextricably mingled that we accept everything with sad pleasure, and smile at the poems' foreknowing, foredefeated, mocking, half-acceptant pain. For in the country of the poems wisdom is a poor butterfly dreaming that it is Chuang-tze, and not an opti-

mistic bird of prey; and the greatest single subject of the romantics, pure potentiality, is treated with a classical grace and
composure.

The most important thing to notice about this treatment,
the rhetorical machinery of the poems, is that it is not a method
of forcing intensity, of creating a factitious or at least arbitrary
excitement, as most modern rhetoric is. Instead of listening
through the hands, with closed eyes, as one is sucked deeper and
deeper into the maelstrom, one listens with one's eyes open and
one's head working about as well as it usually works. Most
writers become over-rhetorical when they are insisting on more
emotion than they actually feel or need to feel; Ransom is just
the opposite. He is perpetually insisting, by his detached, mock-
pedantic, wittily complicated tone, that he is not feeling much
at all, not half so much as he really should be feeling—and this
rhetoric becomes over-mannered, too-protective, when there is
not much emotion for him to pretend not to be feeling, and he
keeps on out of habit. Ransom developed this rhetorical machinery—tone, phrasing, properties, and all the rest—primarily
as a way of handling sentiment or emotion without ever seeming
sentimental or over-emotional; as a way of keeping the poem at
the proper aesthetic distance from its subject; and as a way for
the poem to extract from its subject, no matter how unpleasant
or embarrassing, an unembarrassed pleasure. He was writing
in an age in which the most natural feeling of tenderness, happiness, or sorrow was likely to be called sentimental; consequently he needed a self-protective rhetoric as the most brutal
or violent of poets did not—such a poet, on being told that
some poem of his was a delirium of pointless violence, had only

to reply, with a satisfied smile, "Yes, isn't it?" One can say, *very* crudely, that Ransom's poems are produced by the classical, or at worst semi-classical, treatment of romantic subjects. Both the subjects and the treatment of the poems are Impractical, so far as Ransom's war of the worlds (of Feeling and of Power) is concerned; but the Latinity, mixed generality and peculiarity, and mocking precision of the vocabulary, the sharp intelligence of the tone, are always acknowledging or insisting that we can live only by trading with the enemy—that the heart has its reasons, a mighty poor grade of them, too—that the poet himself is an existence away from the Innocent Doves he mourns for.

I suppose that the quality of Ransom's rhetoric—so different from Laforgue's and Corbière's in form, though fairly similar in some of its functions—was suggested by his profession, by Oxford, by the lingering rhetoric of the South, by the tradition of rhetoric in the ministry, and by his own quite classical education and interests. And I imagine that he had before his eyes, as haunting, more-than-embarrassing examples of the direct treatment of sentimental subjects, some of his own early poems. But by the '30's—as you can see from "Prelude to an Evening," in which most of his rhetoric has disappeared—he could afford an exact, grave directness.

Ransom seems in his poems, as most modern poets do not, sympathetic and charming, full of tenderness and affection, wanting the light and sorry for the dark—moral and condemning only when he has to be, not because he wants to be; loving neither the sterner vices nor the sterner virtues. He has the personal seriousness that treats the world as it seems to him, not the solemnity that treats the really important things, the world as everybody knows it is. His poems are full of an affection that cannot help itself, for an innocence that cannot help itself— for the stupid travellers lost in the maze of the world, for the clever travellers lost in the maze of the world. The poems are not a public argument but personal knowledge, personal feeling; and their virtues are the "merely" private virtues—their characters rarely vote, rarely even kill one another, but often fall in love.

The poems have none of that traumatic passion for Authority, any Authority at all, that is one of the most unpleasant things in our particular time and our particular culture. To tell the truth, the poems are out of place in this most Pharisaical of ages: a time that wanted its artists ruins among its ruins, or else signposts pointing from them to some Heavenly or Earthly City as different as possible from everything, everything; a time that damned Gentile and Jew alike for lacking—of all possible things!—the proper relationship to, or appreciation of, Evil; a time that told each random smile that a smile is nothing but repressed hostility, or sexual sublimation, or ignorance, or evasion, or an escape, or Original Sin, or bourgeois complacency, or a hundred other things each worse than the last; a time that had learned, as no other ever had, that it was a time different from all other times, a last age different from all the ages. It tried, with little success, to forgive the poems for having made a small garden, and not a large crater—for having saved no one by joining a Party or attacking a Party, by exposing the shallowness and corruption of our middle-class culture, by maintaining a paradoxical and ecstatic relationship with God, or by doing anything else that one would expect a poem to do. Instead the poems told stories. Stories!

The attitude of the poems is quiet and complicated; it neither satisfied the expectations nor spoke for the causes of any large body of readers. Any of the poems could have been called, "With Mixed Feelings"; and the feelings of most of their readers may have been mixed-up, but they certainly weren't mixed. The poems were so transparently dialectical that no one called them that: they set out both struggling sides of things, saw both as cater-cornered, corrugated, kaleidoscopic mixtures—all their steady states, even, were hardened and habitual struggles of opposites. (Look at "Painted Head," "The Equilibrists," "Spectral Lovers," "Here Lies a Lady," and many other poems, where all this is plain.) Once I took a little girl to a Tarzan movie; and as each new actor, each new cannibal, each new leopard and monkey and crocodile came on the scene, she would whisper to me desperately: "Is that a *good* one? Is that a *bad* one?" This great root-notion, this imperative at the bottom of our beings, is ill satisfied by Ransom's poems, anomalous things that keep whispering to us, "Both"—that keep whispering to us, "Neither." Perhaps it is best to call them, as Winters does, an "ambiguous and unhappy connective" between the "Experimental Generation" and the "Reactionary Generation"; and certainly, to one so precariously assured of certain certainties as Winters, poems that speak of uncertainties with such ambiguous sureness must seem unhappy.

In Ransom's best poems every part is subordinated to the

whole, and the whole is realized with astonishing exactness and thoroughness. Their economy, precision, and restraint give the poems, sometimes, an individual but impersonal perfection; and Ransom's feel for the exact convention of a particular poem, the exact demands of a particular situation, has resulted in poems different from each other and everything else, as unified, individualized, and unchangeable as nursery rhymes. Who could want or imagine anything different in "Here Lies a Lady," in "Captain Carpenter"? They have the composed and inexhaustible ambiguity of things. Some of Ransom's queer fabulous allegories are close, in form, to Kafka's. If you read "Captain Carpenter" (or *Metamorphosis*, for that matter) to a quite uncultivated audience, it will be delighted with what happens but puzzled about what it means—even "Here Lies a Lady," which seems to an ordinarily cultivated reader almost too immediate to be called allegory, is a puzzling joy to such hearers, since the identification between one's own life or lives in general and the "six little spaces of chill and six of burning," the automatic application of the conceit, occurs to them with difficulty. But Ransom's poetry is not "modernist" poetry at all, normally (notice the difference when it becomes so, in "Painted Head"); and it is remarkable how much narrative, dramatic, not-lyric, not-highbrow interest the best poems have.

Sometimes Ransom uses a version of that ironic-familiar treatment of the past that was so common in the '20's, but he uses it for freshness, sensation by shock, and not for "debunking." More often he does the exact opposite, and treats the present—or future or what has no time at all—in terms of a specific past:

Till knowing his need extreme, and his heart pure,
Christ let them dress him his thick chevelure,
And soon his beard was glozed and sweetly scented.

And very often he is mocking, and pretends to discredit, by the extravagance or incongruity of his terms, precisely what he wishes us to realize that we do believe and cannot help believing.

It is interesting to compare one of Ransom's mock-medieval, carefully mannered poems inside a chosen convention, with one of those pieces of music, composed at the same time, which also were set inside some arbitrarily chosen convention out of the past. And this reminds one of Stravinsky's remark that Wagner "made an organ" of his orchestra—which could also mean, interpreted past reason, that in Wagner all the contradictions are synthesized in a sort of transcendental unity of intensity. In Ransom the contradictions are clear, exactly contradictory, not fused in arbitrary over-all emotion; one admires the clear, sharp, Mozartian lightness of texture of the best poems. And occasionally their phrasing is magical—light as air, soft as dew, the real old-fashioned enchantment:

Go and ask Robin to bring the girls over
To Sweetwater, said my Aunt; and that was why
It was like a dream of ladies sweeping by
The willows, clouds, deep meadowgrass, and the river.

Robin's sisters and my Aunt's lily daughter
Laughed and talked, and tinkled light as wrens
If there were a little colony all hens
To go walking by the steep turn of Sweetwater.

Let them alone, dear Aunt, just for one minute
Till I go fishing in the dark of my mind:
Where have I seen before, against the wind,
These bright virgins, robed and bare of bonnet,

Flowing with music of their strange quick tongue
And adventuring with delicate paces by the stream,—
Myself a child, old suddenly at the scream
From one of the white throats which it hid among?

Not Nausicaa, not Pharaoh's daughter bending among the rushes, gazed with a purer astonishment.

It seems to me that Ransom's best poems are "Captain Carpenter," "Antique Harvesters," "Painted Head," "Here Lies a Lady," "Judith of Bethulia," "Janet Waking," "Prelude to an Evening," "Bells for John Whiteside's Daughter," "Dead Boy," "Tom Tom the Piper's Son," "Vision by Sweetwater," and "Old Mansion." Besides these, "The Equilibrists," "Necrological," and "Armageddon" are elaborately mannered but fairly successful poems of an odd kind; the new version of "Vaunting Oak" has kept all the charm of the old, and has got rid of most of its embarrassing pieces of mannerism and rhetoric; and "Piazza Piece" and "Lady Lost" are good examples of Ransom's microscopic successes. (What beautiful *lieder* five or six of Ransom's poems would make!) And the last stanzas of "Puncture" and "Conrad in Twilight" are plainly Ransom at his best.

Only one of the poems I have mentioned—"Vision by Sweetwater"—is omitted from the *Selected Poems*. One can imagine Ransom's "Mighty slight, mighty slight" as he left it out, but this was a real mistake, the only important mistake in the book. Few poets have ever picked their own best poems so surely, or disliked their weak or impossibly mannered poems so effectively: the whole *Selected Poems* is a little triumph of omission and re- vision, a piece of criticism that makes a great deal of the criticism one might otherwise write entirely unnecessary. (Why condemn a poem, or turn up one's nose at a phrase, that the poet has already omitted or replaced? This implicit criticism of his own poetry is superior to any of Ransom's overt criticism of other people's.) Perhaps "Her Eyes," "Survey of Literature," and "Dog" might have been replaced. "Survey of Literature" is a fairly popular poem, but it seems to me no more than a recipe, a few half-fleshed-out rhymes, and a moral. "Then there was poor Willie Blake/ He foundered on sweet cake" is so queer a judgment, about a poet whose favorite word was *howl*, that one decides it is not a judgment but a rhyme. And "Dog" reminds one of what Goldsmith said about the way Johnson's little fishes would have talked—though here, of course, they are parodying themselves on purpose.

A good many people, wondering what Ransom's poems grew out of, must have gone back to the book he published in 1918. At first reading *Poems About God* is shockingly, almost impos- sibly different from Ransom's later poetry. (Though in the opening poem one comes upon *escheat*, the word that, along with its backward brother *estopped*, was later to become the "little phrase of Vinteuil's" or national anthem of the Fugitives.) Most of the time one is bumping over the furrows of a crude, broad, direct, Southern pastoral, full of reapers and sermons and blackberry pie, quite as country as anything in the early

Frost. Many people might recognize, in "Hurrying home on a windy night/ And hearing tree-tops rubbed and tossed," the familiar accents of a marginal Arcadia; but who would suppose them Ransom's? Most of the earlier *Poems About God* are old-fashioned, amateurishly direct jobs that remind you of the Longfellow-Whittier-Lowell section in your sixth grade reader, and there are a few surprisingly close to popular doggerel: "There's a patch of trees at the edge of the field/ And a brown little house that is kept so warm. . . ." A poem about a practical farmer who, by cutting away the roses at the edge of his field, always got a bigger yield than his neighbors has a name like a steam-roller: "One Who Rejected Christ." But along with the raw innocence of some of the poems there is the raw knowledge that replaces innocence: the "hulk of heaving meat" that "in his vomit laid him down" to die. Some of these earlier poems are nothing but the revulsion and condemnation that are the direct response of innocence and goodness to the evil of the world: at first one is separated from the other absolutely, but afterwards, occasionally, they begin to be joined in the sweet-sour, good-and-evil, steady struggle of opposites that is usual in Ransom's mature poems. The practical and impractical are already at their war: the swimmer floating far down in the cool green depths, with no more need of senses, work, wife, life itself, hears the scolding watch of the world tick grimmer and grimmer, "O *wicked* swimmer!" The preacher being resolutely Christian at Christmas to the little daughter who impatiently says, "I know, I know," begs her father to talk about Santa Claus, and at last weeps, defeated—this is the first of many such poems about children, the first of many such defeats by the world of morals, business, and science. And in "Prayer," when God groans despairingly over the prayers of a poor old woman, several seraphim forget their harping to scold: "O what a wicked woman,/ To shrew his splendid features out of shape!"

"The Power of God" is the first poem to have some of Ransom's elaborate Biblical-pedantic rhetoric; but in many of the poems one can already see his characteristic use of the situation or tone or *gestalt* of the ballad or fairy tale. One smiles at the plain broad beginning of his many-branched myth of Woman: "I have seen women by these bad roads,/ Thank God for that"; but in the poems at the back of the book one finds very different things; and, remembering "Antique Harvesters," one smiles delightedly at Ransom's sympathetic and mocking account of that young Hellenist in Tennessee who

> *Cursed the paternity that planted me*
> *One green leaf in a wilderness of autumn;*
> *And wept, as fitting such a fruitful spirit*
> *Sealed in a yellow tomb.*

One realizes, "Why, it wasn't a mutation—this is Ransom after all"; one has not only seen some of the cruder attitudes, afterwards refined or contradicted, that underlie the later poems, one has wound up in the later poems.

Ransom's poetry shows no individual influences of any real importance. (The Bible, fairy tales, and such are important general influences.) Once, in the early "Geometry," Ransom rewrote Hardy in Hardy's own language: "Unprofited by the centuries/ He still plants on as crazily/ As in his drivelling infancy." And the beginning of "Night Voices," from Ransom's second book, is Hardy being Biblical. Occasionally in *Poems About God* there is a slight flavor of Robinson; and "Tom Tom the Piper's Son" is a working out of a Robinson theme with more grace, concentration, and purity than Robinson could have brought to it himself. Ransom must be almost the only person in the world who has been influenced (though too slightly to talk about, except for fun) by both early and late Yeats: so that as one reads, in *Poems About God,*

> *Must I confess before the pack*
> *Of babblers, idiots, and such?*

one remembers a couple of late-Yeats phrases in Ransom's "Address to the Scholars of New England." But when one reads, in "Old Mansion," the phrases "we beautifully trusted" and "with my happier angel's own temerity," one decides that this is a natural similarity, not simply James.

Ransom has noticeably influenced at least three good poets: Robert Graves, Allen Tate, and Robert Penn Warren. But all three were influenced more by his accident than by his essence, and their best poems show no trace of him. To expect Tate's and Warren's poems to be much influenced by Ransom's is like expecting two nightmares to be influenced by a daydream; and Graves, who might have been more affected, ended with a style all his own only after undergoing considerably more mesmeric American influences.

As Blake said, there is no competition between true poets. Ransom is plainly a member of that strange wonderful family, with about as much individual difference and as much family likeness as is common; and his poems profess their limitations so candidly, almost as a principle of style, that it is hardly necessary to say they are not poems of the largest scope or of the greatest intensity. But it is only fair to say that Ransom is one of the best, most original, and most sympathetic poets alive; and it is easy to see that his poetry will always be cared for, since he has written poems that are perfectly realized and occasionally almost perfect—poems that the hypothetical generations of the future will be reading page by page with Wyatt, Campion, Marvell, and Mother Goose.

But one hates to end on such a grave yew-like note, and had rather cover the last page with a picture, a recollected Breughelish landscape of the country of Ransom's poems. In the center of everything—but unseen, like the blind spot in the middle of one's eye—is the practical world of business and science and morality, a vortex that is laboring to suck everything into its transforming revolutions. In the foreground there is a girl weeping for a dead pet; or simply a girl, dead; and her parents are mourning—in their dry, wistful, pedantic way, full of sentiment and knowledge—this pure potentiality which they have tried helplessly to shelter, but which existence itself has brought to nothing. Nearby the girl, grown up now, stands under the great hollow oak that whispers gently to its daughter —stands torn with pure love, pure pain, as she watches the "serpent's track" of the bicyclist pumping his winding way uphill, carrying the last of all letters to her lover: who walks with blank bitter dryness through the bare wet woods, slashing with a cane at weeds, full of abstraction, morality, and baffled oblivious non-attachedness, a man who has seen through everything except the process of seeing through everything. Children are playing in the vacant lots, animals are playing in the forest. Everything that the machine at the center could not attract or transform it has forced out into the suburbs, the country, the wilderness, the past: out there are the fairy tales and nursery rhymes, chances and choices, dreams and sentiments and intrinsic aesthetic goods—everything that doesn't pay and doesn't care. Out there are the old men, like children now—the defeated Way of an old world—and the gods of that way: Christ and Anti-Christ arming themselves for their tourney; Lamb and Paraclete and Exegete; the friar poring doubtfully over the bloody leaves of the battlefield; Grimes, the old scapegoat, old campaigner, hardened and professional in the habit of atonement, careless of those he dies for:

> Blue blazed the eyes of Grimes in the old manner,—
> The flames of eyes which jewel the head of youth
> Were strange in the leathery phiz of the old campaigner,—
> Smoke and a dry word crackled from his mouth
> And the wind ferried them South.

And there are beauties dangerous as Judith of Bethulia, tender-hearted plant-loving spinsters, lovers embracing like acrobats on a tight-rope, lovers quarreling and wandering through the dewy night like ghosts. Out there are things queer and unchangeable as anything in Grimm: a Quixote who loses on his quests arms, legs, eyes, everything but his tongue and the "old heart in his bust"—and at last those; Tom Tom the Piper's Son, the changeling pulling his little black coat tight about him, glaring around with little grey eyes; the Maiden accosted among the roses of the trellis of the piazza by Death, who has come for her in a dustcoat; the "fine woman" turned into a timid lady bird; the lady whose life was "six little spaces of chill and six of burning . . ." Was she not lucky? Here is old Robert Crocodile: who went to Oxford, carried an umbrella, turned into a society psychoanalyst—an echoingly metaphysical one—and at last sank back into the ooze of the Ohio Everglades, where to this day "floating he lies extended many a rood" among all his kinsfolk.

Some Lines from Whitman

WHITMAN, Dickinson, and Melville seem to me the best poets of the 19th Century here in America. Melville's poetry has been grotesquely underestimated, but of course it is only in the last four or five years that it has been much read; in the long run, in spite of the awkwardness and amateurishness of so much of it, it will surely be thought well of. (In the short run it will probably be thought entirely too well of. Melville is a great poet only in the prose of *Moby Dick.*) Dickinson's poetry has been thoroughly read, and well though undifferentiatingly loved—after a few decades or centuries almost everybody will be able to see through Dickinson to her poems. But something odd has happened to the living changing part of Whitman's reputation: nowadays it is people who are not particularly interested in poetry, people who say that they read a poem for what it says, not for how it says it, who admire Whitman most. Whitman is often written about, either approvingly or disapprovingly, as if he were the Thomas Wolfe of 19th Century democracy, the

SOME LINES FROM WHITMAN

hero of a de Mille movie about Walt Whitman. (People even talk about a war in which Walt Whitman and Henry James chose up sides, to begin with, and in which you and I will go on fighting till the day we die.) All this sort of thing, and all the bad poetry that there of course is in Whitman—for any poet has written enough bad poetry to scare away anybody—has helped to scare away from Whitman most "serious readers of modern poetry." They do not talk of his poems, as a rule, with any real liking or knowledge. Serious readers, people who are ashamed of not knowing all Hopkins by heart, are not at all ashamed to say, "I don't really know Whitman very well." This may harm Whitman in your eyes, they know, but that is a chance that poets have to take. Yet "their" Hopkins, that good critic and great poet, wrote about Whitman, after seeing five or six of his poems in a newspaper review: "I may as well say what I should not otherwise have said, that I always knew in my heart Walt Whitman's mind to be more like my own than any other man's living. As he is a very great scoundrel this is not a very pleasant confession." And Henry James, the leader of "their" side in that awful imaginary war of which I spoke, once read Whitman to Edith Wharton (much as Mozart used to imitate, on the piano, the organ) with such power and solemnity that both sat shaken and silent; it was after this reading that James expressed his regret at Whitman's "too extensive acquaintance with the foreign languages." Almost all the most "original and advanced" poets and critics and readers of the last part of the 19th Century thought Whitman as original and advanced as themselves, in manner as well as in matter. Can Whitman really be a sort of Thomas Wolfe or Carl Sandburg or Robinson Jeffers or Henry

Miller—or a sort of Balzac of poetry, whose every part is crude but whose whole is somehow great? He is not, nor could he be; a poem, like Pope's spider, "lives along the line," and all the dead lines in the world will not make one live poem. As Blake says, "all sublimity is founded on minute discrimination," and it is in these "minute particulars" of Blake's that any poem has its primary existence.

To show Whitman for what he is one does not need to praise or explain or argue, one needs simply to quote. He himself said, "I and mine do not convince by arguments, similes, rhymes,/ We convince by our presence." Even a few of his phrases are enough to show us that Whitman was no sweeping rhetorician, but a poet of the greatest and oddest delicacy and originality and sensitivity, so far as words are concerned. This is, after all, the poet who said, "Blind loving wrestling touch, sheath'd hooded sharp-tooth'd touch"; who said, "Smartly attired, countenance smiling, form upright, death under the breast-bones, hell under the skull-bones"; who said, "Agonies are one of my changes of garments"; who saw grass as the "flag of my disposition," saw "the sharp-peak'd farmhouse, with its scallop'd scum and slender shoots from the gutters," heard a plane's "wild ascending lisp," and saw and heard how at the amputation "what is removed drops horribly in a pail." This is the poet for whom the sea was "howler and scooper of storms," reaching out to us with "crooked inviting fingers"; who went "leaping chasms with a pike-pointed staff, clinging to topples of brittle and blue"; who, a runaway slave, saw how "my gore dribs, thinn'd with the ooze of my skin"; who went "lithographing Kronos . . . buying drafts of Osiris"; who stared out at the "little plentiful mannikins skipping around in collars and tail'd coats,/ I am aware who they are, (they are positively not worms or fleas)." For he is, at his best, beautifully witty: he says gravely, "I find I incorporate gneiss, coals, long-threaded moss, fruits, grain, esculent roots,/ And am stucco'd with quadrupeds and birds all over"; and of these quadrupeds and birds "not one is respectable or unhappy over the whole earth." He calls advice: "Unscrew the locks from the doors! Unscrew the doors from their jambs!" He publishes the results of research: "Having pried through the strata, analyz'd to a hair, counsel'd with doctors and calculated close,/ I find no sweeter fat than sticks to my own bones." Everybody remembers how he told the Muse to "cross out please those immensely overpaid accounts,/ That matter of Troy and Achilles' wrath, and Aeneas', Odysseus' wanderings," but his account of the arrival of the "illustrious emigré" here in the New World is even better: "Bluff'd not a bit by drainpipe, gasometer, artificial fertilizers,/ Smiling and pleas'd with palpable intent to stay,/ She's here, install'd amid the kitchenware." Or he sees, like another Breughel, "the mechanic's wife with the babe at her nipple interceding for every person born,/ Three scythes at harvest whizzing in a row from three lusty angels with shirts bagg'd out at their waists,/ The snag-toothed hostler with red hair redeeming sins past and to come"—the passage has enough wit not only (in Johnson's phrase) to keep it sweet, but enough to make it believable. He says:

I project my hat, sit shame-faced, and beg.

Enough! Enough! Enough!
Somehow I have been stunn'd. Stand back!

Give me a little time beyond my cuff'd head, slumbers,
dreams, gaping,
I discover myself on the verge of a usual mistake.

There is in such changes of tone as these the essence of wit. And Whitman is even more far-fetched than he is witty; he can say about Doubters, in the most improbable and explosive of juxta-positions: "I know every one of you, I know the sea of torment, doubt, despair and unbelief./ How the flukes splash! How they contort rapid as lightning, with splashes and spouts of blood!" Who else would have said about God: "As the hugging and loving bed-fellow sleeps at my side through the night, and with-draws at the break of day with stealthy tread,/ Leaving me bas-kets cover'd with white towels, swelling the house with their plenty"?—the Psalmist himself, his cup running over, would have looked at Whitman with dazzled eyes. (Whitman was persuaded by friends to hide the fact that it was God he was talking about.) He says, "Flaunt of the sunshine I need not your bask—lie over!" This unusual employment of verbs is usual enough in participle-loving Whitman, who also asks you to "look in my face while I snuff the sidle of evening," or tells you, "I effuse my flesh in eddies, and drift it in lacy jags." Here are some typical beginnings of poems: "City of orgies, walks, and joys. . . . Not heaving from my ribb'd breast only. . . . O take my hand Walt Whitman! Such gliding wonders! Such sights and sounds! Such join'd unended links. . . ." He says to the objects of the world, "You have waited, you always wait, you dumb, beautiful ministers"; sees "the sun and stars that float in the open air,/ The apple-shaped earth"; says, "O suns— O grass of graves— O perpetual transfers and promotions,/ If you do not say anything how can I say anything?" Not many poets have written better, in queerer and more convincing and more individual language, about the world's *gliding wonders:* the phrase seems particularly right for Whitman. He speaks of those "circling rivers the breath," of the "savage old mother incessantly crying,/ To the boy's soul's questions sullenly timing, some drown'd secret hissing"— ends a poem, once, "We have voided all but freedom and our own joy." How can one quote enough? If the reader thinks that all this is like Thomas Wolfe he *is* Thomas Wolfe; nothing else could explain it. Poetry like this is as far as possible from the work of any ordinary rhetorician, whose phrases cascade over us like suds of the oldest and most-advertised detergent.

The interesting thing about Whitman's worst language (for, just as few poets have ever written better, few poets have ever written worse) is how unusually absurd, how really ingeniously bad, such language is. I will quote none of the most famous examples; but even a line like *O culpable! I acknowledge. I exposé!* is not anything that you and I could do—only a man with the most extraordinary feel for language, or none whatsoever, could have cooked up Whitman's worst messes. For instance: what other man in all the history of this planet would have said, "I am a habitan of Vienna"? (One has an immediate vision of him as a sort of French-Canadian halfbreed to whom the Viennese are offering, with trepidation, through the bars of a zoological garden, little mounds of whipped cream.) And *enclaircise*—why, it's as bad as *explicate!* We are right to resent his having made up his own horrors, instead of sticking to the ones that we ourselves employ. But when Whitman says, "I dote on myself, there is that lot of me and all so luscious," we should realize that we are not the only ones who are amused. And the queerly bad and merely queer and queerly good will often change into one another without warning: "Hefts of the moving world, at innocent gambols silently rising, freshly exuding,/ Scooting obliquely high and low"—not good, but *queer!*—suddenly becomes, "Something I cannot see puts up libidinous prongs,/ Seas of bright juice suffuse heaven," and it is sunrise.

But it is not in individual lines and phrases, but in passages of some length, that Whitman is at his best. In the following quotation Whitman has something difficult to express, something that there are many formulas, all bad, for expressing; he expresses it with complete success, in language of the most dazzling originality:

> *The orchestra whirls me wider than Uranus flies,*
> *It wrenches such ardors from me I did not know I*
> *   possess'd them,*
> *It sails me, I dab with bare feet, they are lick'd by the*
> *   indolent waves,*
> *I am cut by bitter and angry hail, I lose my breath,*
> *Steep'd amid honey'd morphine, my windpipe throttled in*
> *   fakes of death,*
> *At length let up again to feel the puzzle of puzzles,*
> *And that we call Being.*

One hardly knows what to point at—everything works. But *wrenches* and *did not know I possess'd them;* the incredible *it sails me, I dab with bare feet; lick'd by the indolent; steep'd amid honey'd*

morphine; my windpipe throttled in fakes of death—no wonder
Crane admired Whitman! This originality, as absolute in its
way as that of Berlioz' orchestration, is often at Whitman's
command:

> *I am a dance—play up there! the fit is whirling me fast!*
>
> *I am the ever-laughing—it is new moon and twilight,*
> *I see the hiding of douceurs, I see nimble ghosts whichever*
>   *way I look,*
> *Cache and cache again deep in the ground and sea, and*
>   *where it is neither ground nor sea.*
> *Well do they do their jobs those journeymen divine,*
> *Only from me can they hide nothing, and would not if they*
>   *could,*
> *I reckon I am their boss and they make me a pet besides,*
> *And surround me and lead me and run ahead when I walk,*
> *To lift their sunning covers to signify me with stretch'd arms,*
>   *and resume the way;*
> *Onward we move, a gay gang of blackguards! with mirth-*
>   *shouting music and wild-flapping pennants of joy!*

If you did not believe Hopkins' remark about Whitman, that
gay gang of blackguards ought to shake you. Whitman shares
Hopkins' passion for "dappled" effects, but he slides in and out
of them with ambiguous swiftness. And he has at his command
a language of the calmest and most prosaic reality, one that
seems to do no more than present:

> *The little one sleeps in its cradle.*
> *I lift the gauze and look a long time, and silently brush away*
>   *flies with my hand.*

*The youngster and the red-faced girl turn aside up the bushy
    hill,*
I peeringly view them from the top.

The suicide sprawls on the bloody floor of the bedroom.
*I witness the corpse with its dabbled hair, I note where the
    pistol has fallen.*

It is like magic: that is, something has been done to us without
our knowing how it was done; but if we look at the lines again
we see the *gauze, silently, youngster, red-faced, bushy, peeringly,
dabbled*—not that this is all we see. "Present! present!" said
James; these are presented, put down side by side to form a little
"view of life," from the cradle to the last bloody floor of the
bedroom. Very often the things presented form nothing but a
list:

The pure contralto sings in the organ loft,
*The carpenter dresses his plank, the tongue of his foreplane
    whistles its wild ascending lisp,*
*The married and unmarried children ride home to their
    Thanksgiving dinner,*
*The pilot seizes the king-pin, he heaves down with a strong
    arm,*
*The mate stands braced in the whale-boat, lance and harpoon
    are ready,*
The duck-shooter walks by silent and cautious stretches,
The deacons are ordain'd with cross'd hands at the altar,
*The spinning-girl retreats and advances to the hum of the big
    wheel,*

The farmer stops by the bars as he walks on a First-day loafe
    and looks at the oats and rye,
The lunatic is carried at last to the asylum a confirm'd case,
(He will never sleep any more as he did in the cot in his
    mother's bed-room;)
The jour printer with gray head and gaunt jaws works at his
    case,
He turns his quid of tobacco while his eyes blur with the
    manuscript,
The malform'd limbs are tied to the surgeon's table,
What is removed drops horribly in a pail; . . .

It is only a list—but what a list! And how delicately, in what different ways—likeness and opposition and continuation and climax and anticlimax—the transitions are managed, whenever Whitman wants to manage them. Notice them in the next quotation, another "mere list":

The bride unrumples her white dress, the minute-hand of the
    clock moves slowly,
The opium-eater reclines with rigid head and just-open'd lips,
The prostitute draggles her shawl, her bonnet bobs on her
    tipsy and pimpled neck. . . .

The first line is joined to the third by *unrumples* and *draggles*, *white dress* and *shawl;* the second to the third by *rigid head*, *bobs, tipsy, neck;* the first to the second by *slowly, just-open'd*, and the slowing-down of time in both states. And occasionally one of these lists is metamorphosed into something we have no name for; the man who would call the next quotation a mere list—anybody will feel this—would boil his babies up for soap:

Ever the hard unsunk ground,
Ever the eaters and drinkers, ever the upward and downward
  sun,
Ever myself and my neighbors, refreshing, wicked, real,
Ever the old inexplicable query, ever that thorned thumb, that
  breath of itches and thirsts,
Ever the vexer's hoot! hoot! till we find where the sly one hides
  and bring him forth,
Ever the sobbing liquid of life,
Ever the bandage under the chin, ever the trestles of death.

Sometimes Whitman will take what would generally be considered an unpromising subject (in this case, a woman peeping at men in bathing naked) and treat it with such tenderness and subtlety and understanding that we are ashamed of ourselves for having thought it unpromising, and murmur that Chekhov himself couldn't have treated it better:

Twenty-eight young men bathe by the shore,
Twenty-eight young men and all so friendly,
Twenty-eight years of womanly life and all so lonesome.

She owns the fine house by the rise of the bank,
She hides handsome and richly drest aft the blinds of the
  window.

Which of the young men does she like the best?
Ah the homeliest of them is beautiful to her.

Where are you off to, lady? for I see you,
You splash in the water there, yet stay stock still in your room.

Dancing and laughing along the beach came the twenty-ninth
    bather,
The rest did not see her, but she saw them and loved them.

The beards of the young men glistened with wet, it ran from
    their long hair,
Little streams pass'd all over their bodies.

An unseen hand also pass'd over their bodies,
It descended tremblingly from their temples and ribs.

The young men float on their backs, their white bellies bulge
    to the sun, they do not ask who seizes fast to them,
They do not know who puffs and declines with pendant and
    bending arch,
They do not know whom they souse with spray.

And in the same poem (that "Song of Myself" in which one
finds half his best work) the writer can say of a sea-fight:

Stretched and still lies the midnight,
Two great hulls motionless on the breast of the darkness,
Our vessel riddled and slowly sinking, preparations to pass
    to the one we have conquer'd,
The captain on the quarter-deck coldly giving his orders
    through a countenance white as a sheet,
Near by the corpse of the child that serv'd in the cabin,
The dead face of an old salt with long white hair and carefully
    curl'd whiskers,
The flames spite of all that can be done flickering aloft and
    below,

The husky voices of the two or three officers yet fit for duty,
Formless stacks of bodies and bodies by themselves, dabs of
flesh upon the masts and spars,
Cut of cordage, dangle of rigging, slight shock of the soothe of
waves,
Black and impassive guns, litter of powder-parcels, strong
scent,
A few large stars overhead, silent and mournful shining,
Delicate snuffs of sea-breeze, smells of sedgy grass and fields by
the shore, death-messages given in charge to survivors,
The hiss of the surgeon's knife, the gnawing teeth of his saw,
Wheeze, cluck, swash of falling blood, short wild scream, and
long, dull, tapering groan,
These so, these irretrievable.

There are faults in this passage, and they *do not matter:* the serious truth, the complete realization of these last lines make us remember that few poets have shown more of the tears of things, and the joy of things, and of the reality beneath either tears or joy. Even Whitman's most general or political statements sometimes are good: everybody knows his "When liberty goes out of a place it is not the first to go, nor the second or third to go,/ It waits for all the rest to go, it is the last"; these sentences about the United States just before the Civil War may be less familiar:

Are those really Congressmen? are those the great Judges?
is that the President?
Then I will sleep awhile yet, for I see that these States sleep,
for reasons;

(*With gathering murk, with muttering thunder and lambent
    shoots we all duly awake,*
*South, North, East, West, inland and seaboard, we will surely
    awake.*)

How well, with what firmness and dignity and command, Whitman does such passages! And Whitman's doubts that he has done them or anything else well—ah, there is nothing he does better:

The best I had done seemed to me blank and suspicious,
*My great thoughts as I supposed them, were they not in reality
    meagre?*
I am he who knew what it was to be evil,
I too knitted the old knot of contrariety . . .
*Saw many I loved in the street or ferry-boat or public assembly,
    yet never told them a word,*
*Lived the same life with the rest, the same old laughing,
    gnawing, sleeping,*
Played the part that still looks back on the actor and actress,
The same old role, the role that is what we make it . . .

Whitman says once that the "look of the bay mare shames silliness out of me." This is true—sometimes it is true; but more often the silliness and affection and cant and exaggeration are there shamelessly, the Old Adam that was in Whitman from the beginning and the awful new one that he created to keep it company. But as he says, "I know perfectly well my own egotism,/ Know my omnivorous lines and must not write any less." He says over and over that there are in him good and bad, wise and foolish, anything at all and its antonym, and he is telling the truth; there is in him almost everything in the world, so that one responds to him, willingly or unwillingly, almost as one does to the world, that world which makes the hairs of one's flesh stand up, which seems both evil beyond any rejection and wonderful beyond any acceptance. We cannot help seeing that there is something absurd about any judgment we make of its whole—for there is no "point of view" at which we can stand to make the judgment, and the moral categories that mean most to us seem no more to apply to its whole than our spatial or temporal or causal categories seem to apply to its beginning or its end. (But we need no arguments to make our judgments seem absurd—we feel their absurdity without argument.) In some like sense Whitman is a world, a waste with, here and there, systems blazing at random out of the darkness. Only an innocent and rigidly methodical mind will reject it for this disorganization, particularly since there are in it, here and there, little systems as beautifully and astonishingly organized as the rings and satellites of Saturn:

> *I understand the large hearts of heroes,*
> *The courage of present times and all times,*
> *How the skipper saw the crowded and rudderless wreck of the*
> *steam-ship, and Death chasing it up and down the storm,*
> *How he knuckled tight and gave not back an inch, and was*
> *faithful of days and faithful of nights,*
> *And chalked in large letters on a board, Be of good cheer, we*
> *will not desert you;*
> *How he follow'd with them and tack'd with them three days and*
> *would not give it up,*

How he saved the drifting company at last,
How the lank loose-gown'd women looked when boated from
the side of their prepared graves,
How the silent old-faced infants and the lifted sick, and the
sharp-lipp'd unshaved men;
All this I swallow, it tastes good, I like it well, it becomes mine,
I am the man, I suffered, I was there.

In the last lines of this quotation Whitman has reached—as great writers always reach—a point at which criticism seems not only unnecessary but absurd: these lines are so good that even admiration feels like insolence, and one is ashamed of anything that one can find to say about them. How anyone can dismiss or accept patronizingly the man who wrote them, I do not understand.

The enormous and apparent advantages of form, of omission and selection, of the highest degree of organization, are accompanied by important disadvantages—and there are far greater works than *Leaves of Grass* to make us realize this. But if we compare Whitman with that very beautiful poet Alfred Tennyson, the most skillful of all Whitman's contemporaries, we are at once aware of how limiting Tennyson's forms have been, of how much Tennyson has had to leave out, even in those discursive poems where he is trying to put everything in. Whitman's poems *represent* his world and himself much more satisfactorily than Tennyson's do his. In the past a few poets have both formed and represented, each in the highest degree; but in modern times what controlling, organizing, selecting poet has created a world with as much in it as Whitman's, a world that so plainly *is* the world? Of all modern poets he has, quantitatively speaking, "the most comprehensive soul"—and, qualitatively, a most comprehensive and comprehending one, with charities and concessions and qualifications that are rare in any time.

"Do I contradict myself? Very well then I contradict myself," wrote Whitman, as everybody remembers, and this is not naive, or something he got from Emerson, or a complacent pose. When you organize one of the contradictory elements out of your work of art, you are getting rid not just of it, but of the contradiction of which it was a part; and it is the contradictions in works of art which make them able to represent to us—as logical and methodical generalizations cannot—our world and our selves, which are also full of contradictions. In Whitman we do not get the controlled, compressed, seemingly concordant contradictions of the great lyric poets, of a poem like, say, Hardy's "During Wind and Rain"; Whitman's contradictions are sometimes announced openly, but are more often scattered at random throughout the poems. For instance: Whitman specializes in ways of saying that there is in some sense (a very Hegelian one, generally) no evil—he says a hundred times that evil is not Real; but he also specializes in making lists of the evil of the world, lists of an unarguable reality. After his minister has recounted "the rounded catalogue divine complete," Whitman comes home and puts down what has been left out: "the countless (nineteen-twentieths) low and evil, crude and savage . . . the barren soil, the evil men, the slag and hideous rot." He ends another such catalogue with the plain unexcusing "All these—all meanness and agony without end I sitting look out upon,/ See, hear, and am silent." Whitman offered himself to everybody,

and said brilliantly and at length what a good thing he was
offering:

> Sure as the most certain sure, plumb in the uprights,
>   well entretied, braced in the beams,
> Stout as a horse, affectionate, haughty, electrical,
> I and this mystery here we stand.

Just for oddness, characteristicalness, differentness, what more
could you ask in a letter of recommendation? (Whitman sounds
as if he were recommending a house—haunted, but what founda-
tions!) But after a few pages he is oddly different:

> Apart from the pulling and hauling stands what I am,
> Stands amused, complacent, compassionating, idle, unitary,
> Looks down, is erect, or bends an arm on an impalpable certain
>   rest
> Looking with side curved head curious what will come next,
> Both in and out of the game and watching and wondering at it.

Tamburlaine is already beginning to sound like Hamlet: the em-
ployer feels uneasily, "Why, I might as well hire myself. . . ."
And, a few pages later, Whitman puts down in ordinary-sized
type, in the middle of the page, this warning to any *new person
drawn toward me:*

> Do you think I am trusty and faithful?
> Do you see no further than this façade, this smooth and
>   tolerant manner of me?
> Do you suppose yourself advancing on real ground to-
>   ward a real heroic man?

Have you no thought O dreamer that it may be all maya,
illusion?

Having wonderful dreams, telling wonderful lies, was a temptation Whitman could never resist; but telling the truth was a
temptation he could never resist, either. When you buy him you
know what you are buying. And only an innocent and solemn
and systematic mind will condemn him for his contradictions:
Whitman's catalogues of evils represent realities, and his denials
of their reality represent other realities, of feeling and intuition
and desire. If he is faithless to logic, to Reality As It Is—whatever that is—he is faithful to the feel of things, to reality as it
seems; this is all that a poet has to be faithful to, and philosophers have been known to leave logic and Reality for it.

Whitman is more coordinate and parallel than anybody, is
the poet of parallel present participles, of twenty verbs joined by
a single subject: all this helps to give his work its feeling of raw
hypnotic reality, of being that world which also streams over us
joined only by *ands*, until we supply the subordinating conjunctions; and since as children we see the *ands* and not the *becauses*,
this method helps to give Whitman some of the freshness of
childhood. How inexhaustibly interesting the world is in Whitman! Arnold all his life kept wishing that he could see the world
"with a plainness as near, as flashing" as that with which Moses
and Rebekah and the Argonauts saw it. He asked with elegiac
nostalgia, "Who can see the green earth any more/ As she was
by the sources of Time?"—and all the time there was somebody
alive who saw it so, as plain and near and flashing, and with a
kind of calm, pastoral, Biblical dignity and elegance as well,

sometimes. The *thereness* and *suchness* of the world are incarnate in Whitman as they are in few other writers.

They might have put on his tombstone WALT WHITMAN: HE HAD HIS NERVE. He is the rashest, the most inexplicable and unlikely—the most impossible, one wants to say—of poets. He somehow *is* in a class by himself, so that one compares him with other poets about as readily as one compares *Alice* with other books. (Even his free verse has a completely different effect from anybody else's.) Who would think of comparing him with Tennyson or Browning or Arnold or Baudelaire?—it is Homer, or the sagas, or something far away and long ago, that comes to one's mind only to be dismissed; for sometimes Whitman *is* epic, just as *Moby Dick* is, and it surprises us to be able to use truthfully this word that we have misused so many times. Whitman *is* grand, and elevated, and comprehensive, and real with an astonishing reality, and many other things—the critic points at his qualities in despair and wonder, all method failing, and simply calls them by their names. And the range of these qualities is the most extraordinary thing of all. We can surely say about him, "He was a man, take him for all in all. I shall not look upon his like again"—and wish that people had seen this and not tried to be his like: one Whitman is miracle enough, and when he comes again it will be the end of the world.

I have said so little about Whitman's faults because they are so plain: baby critics who have barely learned to complain of the lack of ambiguity in *Peter Rabbit* can tell you all that is wrong with *Leaves of Grass*. But a good many of my readers must have felt that it is ridiculous to write an essay about the obvious fact that Whitman is a great poet. It is ridiculous—just as, in 1851, it would have been ridiculous for anyone to write an essay about the obvious fact that Pope was no "classic of our prose" but a great poet. Critics have to spend half their time reiterating whatever ridiculously obvious things their age or the critics of their age have found it necessary to forget: they say despairingly, at parties, that Wordsworth is a great poet, and *won't* bore you, and tell Mr. Leavis that Milton is a great poet whose deposition *hasn't* been accomplished with astonishing ease by a few words from Eliot. . . . There is something essentially ridiculous about critics, anyway: what is good is good without our saying so, and beneath all our majesty we know this.

Let me finish by mentioning another quality of Whitman's— a quality, delightful to me, that I have said nothing of. If some day a tourist notices, among the ruins of New York City, a copy of *Leaves of Grass*, and stops and picks it up and reads some lines in it, she will be able to say to herself: "How very American! If he and his country had not existed, it would have been impossible to imagine them."

Reflections on Wallace Stevens

LET me begin with a quotation from Stendhal: "'What I find completely lacking in all these people,' thought Lucien, 'is the unexpected. . . .' He was reduced to philosophizing." In my quotation Lucien stands for Stevens, "these people" for America and Business, "the unexpected" for Culture, the exotic, the past, the Earth-minus-America; "philosophizing" stands for, alas! philosophizing. . . . But before Stevens was reduced to it, he drew the unexpected from a hundred springs. There has never been a travel poster like *Harmonium:* how many of its readers must have sold what they had, given the money to steamship agents, and gone to spend the rest of their lives in Lhasa. Yet there was nothing really unusual in what Stevens felt. To have reached, in 1900, in the United States, the age of twenty-one, or fifteen, or twelve—as Stevens and Pound and Eliot did—this was so hard a thing for poets, went so thoroughly against the grain, that they emigrated as soon as they could, or stayed home and wrote poems in which foreignness,

pastness, is itself a final good. "But how absurd!" a part of anyone protests. "Didn't they realize that, to a poet, New York
City means just as much as Troy and Jerusalem and all the
rest of those *immensely overpaid accounts* that Whitman begged
the Muse, *install'd amid the kitchenware*, to cross out?" They
didn't realize it; if one realizes it, one is not a poet. The accounts
have been overpaid too many years for people ever to stop paying; to keep on paying them is to be human. To be willing to
give up Life for the last local slice of it, for all those Sears Roe-
buck catalogues which, as businessmen and generals say, would
be the most effective propaganda we could possibly drop on
the Russians—this is a blinded chauvinism, a provincialism in
space and time, which is even worse than that vulgar exoticism
which disregards both what we have kept and what we are
unique in possessing, which gives up *Moby Dick* for the Journals
of André Gide. Our most disastrous lacks—delicacy, awe, order,
natural magnificence and piety, "the exquisite errors of time,"
and the rest; everything that is neither bought, sold, nor imagined on Sunset Boulevard or in Times Square; everything the
absence of which made Lorca think Hell a city very like New
York—these things were the necessities of Stevens' spirit. Some
of his poems set about supplying these lacks—from other times
and places, from the underlying order of things, from the imagination; other poems look with mockery and despair at the
time and place that cannot supply them, that do not even
desire to supply them; other poems reason or seem to reason
about their loss, about their nature, about their improbable
restoration. His poetry is obsessed with lack, a lack at last almost taken for granted, that he himself automatically supplies;

if sometimes he has restored by imagination or abstraction or re-creation, at other times he has restored by collection, almost as J. P. Morgan did—Stevens likes something, buys it (at the expense of a little spirit), and ships it home in a poem. The feeling of being a leisured, cultivated, and sympathetic tourist (in a time-machine, sometimes) is essential to much of his work; most of his contact with values is at the distance of knowledge and regret—an aesthetician's or an archaeologist's contact with a painting, not a painter's.

Many of Stevens' readers have resented his—so to speak—spending his time collecting old porcelain: "if old things are what you want," they felt, "why don't you collect old Fords or Locomobiles or Stutz Bearcats, or old Mother Bloors, right here at home?" But, for an odd reason, people have never resented the cruel truths or half-truths he told them about the United States. Once upon a time Richard Dehmel's poems, accused of obscenity, were acquitted on the grounds that they were incomprehensible—and almost exactly this happened to Stevens' home-truths. Yet they were plain, sometimes. Looking at General Jackson confronting the "mockers, the mickey mockers," Stevens decided what the "American Sublime" is: the sublime "comes down/ To the spirit itself,/ The spirit and space,/ The empty spirit/ In vacant space." Something like this is true, perhaps, always and everywhere; yet it is a hard truth for your world to have reduced you to: it is no wonder the poem ends, "What wine does one drink?/ What bread does one eat?" And in "The Common Life" the church steeple is a "black line beside a white line," not different in any way from "the stack of the electric plant"; in the "flat air," the "morbid light,"

a man is "a result, a demonstration"; the men "have no shad-
ows/ And the women only one side." We live "no longer on the
ancient cake of seed,/ The almond and deep fruit. . . . We
feast on human heads"; the table is a mirror and the diners eat
reflections of themselves. "The steeples are empty and so are
the people," he says in "Loneliness in Jersey City"; the poem is
full of a despairing frivolity, as Stevens looks from Room 2903
out over that particular countryside which, I think, God once
sent angels to destroy, but which the angels thought worse
than anything they could do to it. And "In Oklahoma,/ Bonnie
and Josie,/ Dressed in calico,/ Danced around a stump./ They
cried,/ 'Ohoyaho,/ Ohoo' . . ./ Celebrating the marriage/
Of flesh and air." Without what's superfluous, the excess of
the spirit, man is a poor, bare, forked animal. In "Country
Words" the poet sits under the willows of exile, and sings "like
a cuckoo clock" to Belshazzar, that "putrid rock,/ putrid pillar
of a putrid people"; he sings "an old rebellious song,/ An edge of
song that never clears." But if it should clear, if the cloud that
hangs over his heart and mind should lift, it would be because
Belshazzar heard and understood:

> What is it that my feeling seeks?
> I know from all the things it touched
> And left beside and left behind.
> It wants the diamond pivot bright.
> It wants Belshazzar reading right
> The luminous pages on his knee,
> Of being, more than birth and death.
> It wants words virile with his breath.

If this intellectual is "isolated," it is not because he wants to
be. . . . But Stevens' most despairing, amusing, and exactly
realized complaint is "Disillusionment of Ten O'Clock":

> *The houses are haunted*
> *By white nightgowns.*
> *None are green,*
> *Or purple with green rings,*
> *Or green with yellow rings,*
> *Or yellow with blue rings.*
> *None of them are strange,*
> *With socks of lace*
> *And beaded ceintures.*
> *People are not going*
> *To dream of baboons and periwinkles.*
> *Only, here and there, an old sailor,*
> *Drunk and asleep in his boots,*
> *Catches tigers*
> *In red weather.*

Any schoolboy (of the superior Macaulayish breed) more or less
feels what this poem means, but it is interesting to look at one
or two details. Why *ten o'clock*? They have all gone to bed early,
like good sensible machines; and the houses' ghosts, now, are
only nightgowns, the plain white nightgowns of the Common
Man, Economic Man, Rational Man—pure commonplace, no
longer either individual or strange or traditional; and the dreams
are as ordinary as the nightgowns. Here and there a drunken
and disreputable *old sailor* still lives in the original reality (he
doesn't dream of catching, he *catches*): *sailor* to bring in old-

fashioned Europe, old-fashioned Asia, the old-fashioned ocean; *old* to bring in the past, to make him a dying survival. What indictment of the Present has ever compared, for flat finality, with "People are not going/ To dream of baboons and periwinkles"? Yet isn't this poem ordinarily considered a rather nonsensical and Learish poem?

It is not until later that Stevens writes much about what America has in common with the rest of the world; then he splits everything differently, and contrasts with the past of America and of the world their present. In *Harmonium* he still loves America best when he can think of it as wilderness, naturalness, pure potentiality (he treats with especial sympathy Negroes, Mexican Indians, and anybody else he can consider wild); and it is this feeling that is behind the conclusion of "Sunday Morning":

> *She hears, upon that water without sound,*
> *A voice that cries, "The tomb in Palestine*
> *Is not the porch of spirits lingering.*
> *It is the grave of Jesus, where he lay."*
> *We live in an old chaos of the sun,*
> *Or old dependency of day and night,*
> *Or island solitude, unsponsored, free,*
> *Of that wide water, inescapable.*
> *Deer walk upon our mountains, and the quail*
> *Whistle about us their spontaneous cries;*
> *Sweet berries ripen in the wilderness;*
> *And, in the isolation of the sky,*
> *At evening, casual flocks of pigeons make*

Ambiguous undulations as they sink
Downward to darkness, on extended wings.

Here—in the last purity and refinement of the grand style, as perfect, in its calm transparency, as the best of Wordsworth—is the last wilderness, come upon so late in the history of mankind that it is no longer seen as the creation of God, but as the Nature out of which we evolve; man without myth, without God, without anything but the universe which has produced him, is given an extraordinarily pure and touching grandeur in these lines—lines as beautiful, perhaps, as any in American poetry. Yet Stevens himself nearly equals them in two or three parts of *Esthétique du Mal,* the best of his later poems; there are in *Harmonium* six or eight of the most beautiful poems an American has written; and a book like *Parts of a World* is delightful as a whole, even though it contains no single poem that can compare with the best in *Harmonium.* But *Auroras of Autumn,* Stevens' last book, is a rather different affair. One sees in it the distinction, intelligence, and easy virtuosity of a master—but it would take more than these to bring to life so abstract, so monotonous, so overwhelmingly *characteristic* a book. Poems like these are, always, the product of a long process of evolution; in Stevens' case the process has been particularly interesting.

The habit of philosophizing in poetry—or of seeming to philosophize, of using a philosophical tone, images, constructions, of having quasi-philosophical daydreams—has been unfortunate for Stevens. Poetry is a bad medium for philosophy.

Everything in the philosophical poem has to satisfy irreconcilable requirements: for instance, the last demand that we should make of philosophy (that it be interesting) is the first we make of a poem; the philosophical poet has an elevated and methodical, but forlorn and absurd air as he works away at his flying tank, his sewing-machine that also plays the piano. (One thinks of Richard Wilbur's graceful "Tom Swift has vanished too,/ Who worked at none but wit's expense,/ Putting dirigibles together,/ Out in the yard, in the quiet weather,/ Whistling behind Tom Sawyer's fence.") When the first thing that Stevens can find to say of the Supreme Fiction is that "it must be *abstract*," the reader protests, "Why, even Hegel called it a *concrete* universal"; the poet's medium, words, is abstract to begin with, and it is only his unique organization of the words that forces the poem, generalizations and all, over into the concreteness and singularity that it exists for. But Stevens has the weakness—a terrible one for a poet, a steadily increasing one in Stevens—of thinking of particulars as primarily illustrations of general truths, or else as aesthetic, abstracted objects, simply there to be contemplated; he often treats things or lives so that they seem no more than generalizations of an unprecedentedly low order. But surely a poet *has* to treat the concrete as primary, as something far more than an instance, a hue to be sensed, a member of a laudable category—for him it is always the generalization whose life is derived, whose authority is delegated. Goethe said, quite as if he were talking about Stevens: "It makes a great difference whether the poet seeks the particular in relation to the universal or contemplates the universal in the particular . . . [In the first case] the particular functions as an example, as an instance of the universal; but the second indeed represents the very nature of poetry. He who grasps this particular as living essence also encompasses the universal."

As a poet Stevens has every gift but the dramatic. It is the lack of immediate contact with lives that hurts his poetry more than anything else, that has made it easier and easier for him to abstract, to philosophize, to treat the living dog that wags its tail and bites you as the "canoid patch" of the epistemologist analyzing that great problem, the world; as the "cylindrical arrangement of brown and white" of the aesthetician analyzing that great painting, the world. Stevens knows better, often for poems at a time:

> At dawn,
>
>> The paratroopers fall and as they fall
>> They mow the lawn. A vessel sinks in waves
>> Of people, as big bell-billows from its bell
>> Bell-bellow in the village steeple. Violets,
>> Great tufts, spring up from buried houses
>> Of poor, dishonest people, for whom the steeple,
>> Long since, rang out farewell, farewell, farewell.

This is a map with people living on it. Yet it is fatally easy for the scale to become too small, the distance too great, and us poor, dishonest people no more than data to be manipulated.

As one reads Stevens' later poetry one keeps thinking that he needs to be possessed by subjects, to be shaken out of himself, to have his subject individualize his poem; one remembers longingly how much more individuation there was in *Harmonium*—when you're young you try to be methodical and philosophical, but reality keeps breaking in. The best of *Harmonium* exists at a level that it is hard to rise above; and Stevens has had only faintly and intermittently the dramatic insight, the capacity to be obsessed by lives, actions, subject-matter, the chameleon's shameless interest in everything but itself, that could have broken up the habit and order and general sobering matter-of-factness of age. Often, nowadays, he seems disastrously set in his own ways, a fossil imprisoned in the rock of himself—the best marble but, still, marble.

All his *tunk-a-tunks*, his *hoo-goo-boos*—those mannered, manufactured, individual, uninteresting little sound-inventions—how typical they are of the lecture-style of the English philosopher, who makes grunts or odd noises, uses homely illustrations, and quotes day in and day out from *Alice*, in order to give what he says some appearance of that raw reality it so plainly and essentially lacks. These "tootings at the wedding of the soul" are fun for the tooter, but get as dreary for the reader as do all the foreign words—a few of these are brilliant, a few more pleasant, and the rest a disaster: "one cannot help deploring his too extensive acquaintance with the foreign languages," as Henry James said, of Walt Whitman, to Edith Wharton.

Stevens is never more philosophical, abstract, rational, than when telling us to put our faith in nothing but immediate sensations, perceptions, aesthetic particulars; for this is only a generalization offered for assent, and where in the ordinary late poem are the real particulars of the world—the people, the acts, the lives—for us to put our faith in? And when Stevens makes a myth to hold together aesthetic particulars and generalizations, it is as if one were revisited by the younger Saint-Simon, Comte, and that actress who played Reason to Robespierre's approving glare; Stevens' myths spring not from the soil but from the clouds, the arranged, scrubbed, reasoning clouds in someone's head. He is too rational and composedly fanciful a being to make up a myth—one could as easily imagine his starting a cult in Los Angeles. When one reads most eighteenth-century writing one is aware of some man of good sense and good taste and good will at the bottom of everything and everybody; but in Stevens—who is always swinging between baroque and rococo, and reminds one of the eighteenth century in dozens of ways—this being at the bottom of everything is cultivated and appreciative and rational out of all reason: the Old Adam in everybody turns out to be not Robinson Crusoe but Bernard Berenson.

Metastasio began as an improviser and ended as a poet; as one reads the average poem in *Auroras of Autumn* one feels that the opposite has been happening to Stevens. A poem begins, revealingly: "An exercise in viewing the world./ On the motive! But one looks at the sea/ As one improvises, on the piano." And not the sea only. One reads a book like this with odd mixed pleasure, not as if one were reading poems but as if one were reading some *Travel-Diary of an Aesthetician*, who works more for pleasure than for truth, puts in entries regularly, and gives one continual pleasure in incidentals, in good phrases, interesting ideas, delicate perceptions, but who hardly tries to subordinate his Method to the requirements of any particular situation or material. The individual poems are less and less differentiated; the process is always more evident than what is being processed; everything is so familiarly contrived by will and habit and rule of thumb (for improvisation, as Virgil Thomson says, "among all the compositional techniques is the one most servile to rules of thumb") that it does not seem to matter exactly which being is undergoing these immemorial metamorphoses. Stevens' passagework, often, is so usual that we can't believe past the form to the matter: what truth could survive these pastry-cook's, spun-sugar, parallel qualifications?

> *It was like sudden time in a world without time,*
> *This world, this place, the street in which I was,*
> *Without time: as that which is not has not time,*
> *Is not, or is of what there was, is full. . . .*

And on the shelf below:

> *It was nowhere else, it was there and because*
> *It was nowhere else, its place had to be supposed,*
> *Itself had to be supposed, a thing supposed*
> *In a place supposed, a thing that reached*
> *In a place that he reached. . . .*

It is G. E. Moore at the spinet. And it looks worst of all when one compares it with a passage from that classic of our prose, that generalizer from an Age of Reason, that hapless victim of Poetic Diction, that—but let me quote:

> *As Hags hold Sabbaths, less for joy than spite,*
> *So these their merry, miserable Night;*
> *Still round and round the Ghosts of Beauty glide,*
> *And haunt the places where their Honor died.*
> *See how the World its Veterans rewards!*
> *A Youth of Frolics, an old Age of Cards;*

Fair to no purpose, artful to no end,
Young without Lovers, old without a Friend;
A Fop their Passion, but their Prize a Sot;
Alive, ridiculous, and dead, forgot!

The immediacy and precision and particularity, the live touch of things, the beauty that exists in precarious perfection in so many poems in *Harmonium*—

> *the beauty*
> *Of the moonlight*
> *Falling there,*
> *Falling*
> *As sleep falls*
> *In the innocent air*—

this, at last, is lost in rhetoric, in elaboration and artifice and contrivance, in an absolutely ecumenical Method of seeing and thinking and expressing, in *craftsmanship:* why has no loving soul ever given Stevens a copy of that *Principles of Art* in which Collingwood argues at length—many people might say *proves*—that art is not a craft at all? (I hardly dare to quote one great poet's even more sweeping "But I deny that poetry is an art.") In *Auroras of Autumn* one sees almost everything through a shining fog, a habitualness not just of style but of machinery, perception, anything: the green spectacles show us a world of green spectacles; and the reader, staring out into this Eden, thinks timidly: "But it's all so *monotonous.*" When Marx said that he wasn't a Marxist he meant, I suppose, that he himself was not one of his own followers, could not be taken in by the prolongation and simplification of his own beliefs that a disciple would make and believe; and there is nothing a successful artist needs to pray so much as: "Lord, don't let me keep on believing *only this;* let me have the courage of something besides my own convictions; let me escape at last from the maze of myself, from the hardening quicksilver womb of my own characteristicalness."

I have felt as free as posterity to talk in this way of Stevens' weaknesses, of this later mold in which he has cast himself, since he seems to me—and seems to my readers, I am sure—one of the true poets of our century, someone whom the world will keep on reading just as it keeps on listening to Vivaldi or Scarlatti, looking at Tiepolo or Poussin. His best poems are the poetry of a man fully human—of someone sympathetic, magnanimous, both brightly and deeply intelligent; the poems see, feel, and think with equal success; they treat with mastery that part of existence which allows of mastery, and experience the rest of it with awe or sadness or delight. Minds of this quality of genius, of this breadth and delicacy of understanding, are a link between us and the past, since they are, for us, the past made living; and they are our surest link with the future, since they are the part of us which the future will know. As one feels the elevation and sweep and disinterestedness, the thoughtful truthfulness of the best sections of a poem like *Esthétique du Mal,* one is grateful for, overawed by, this poetry that knows so well the size and age of the world; that reminds us, as we sit in chairs produced from the furniture exhibitions of the Museum of Modern Art, of that immemorial order or disorder upon which our present scheme of things is a monomolecular film; that counsels us—as Santayana wrote of Spinoza—"to say to those little gnostics, to those circumnavigators of being: *I do not believe you; God is great.*" Many of the poems look greyly out at "the immense detritus of a world/ That is completely waste, that moves from waste/ To waste, out of the hopeless waste of the past/ Into a hopeful waste to come"; but more of the poems see the unspoilable delights, the inexhaustible interests of existence—when you have finished reading Stevens' best poems you remember once more that man is not only the jest and riddle of the world, but the glory.

Some of my readers may feel about all this, "But how can you reconcile what you say with the fact that *Auroras of Autumn* is not a good book? Shouldn't the Mature poet be producing late masterpieces even better than the early ones?" (They might ask the same thing about *The Cocktail Party*.) All such questions show how necessary it is to think of the poet as somebody who has prepared himself to be visited by a daemon, as a sort of accident-prone worker to whom poems happen—for otherwise we *expect* him to go on writing good poems, better poems, and this is the one thing you cannot expect even of good poets, much less of anybody else. Good painters in their sixties may produce good pictures as regularly as an orchard produces apples; but Planck is a great scientist because he made one discovery as a young man—and I can remember reading in a mathematician's memoirs a sentence composedly recognizing the fact that, since the writer was now past forty, he was unlikely ever again to do any important creative work in mathematics. A man who is a good poet at forty *may* turn out to be

a good poet at sixty; but he is more likely to have stopped writing poems, to be doing exercises in his own manner, or to have
reverted to whatever commonplaces were popular when he
was young. A good poet is someone who manages, in a lifetime of standing out in thunderstorms, to be struck by lightning
five or six times; a dozen or two dozen times and he is great.

A Verse Chronicle

I F Y O U ever review for *The Nation* most of the poetry that is being published, what you write will be called a *Verse Chronicle*, so that for an instant you will feel yourself a last successor to Hesiod and Snorri Sturlusson. What I used to write was far from a chronicle, and farther from verse; my short reviews ordinarily grew into long reviews, or short essays, or pieces that were no longer Chronicles at all, but articles in Book Numbers—and Margaret Marshall, more like an angel than an editor, never complained. Here are seven of the Chronicles; I have added several paragraphs to several.

. I.

WHEN A READER finishes Walter de la Mare's new book, *The Burning Glass*, he is amused by how complicated his feelings about it are. To enjoy much of it much, you have to make great

149

concessions, great allowances; yet you feel that you would be a fool not to, that the allowances are ordinary good sense, common politeness. De la Mare is a hopeless romantic? Yes; but whose Law is it that a hopeless romantic cannot write good poetry? Reading de la Mare, one often has a sense of delicate and individual boredom, and wishes him a better writer than he is; but the man who would wish him a *different* writer would wish the Great Snowy Owl at the zoo a goose, so as to eat it for Christmas.

There are two or three beautiful poems in *The Burning Glass;* it is a book which will interest and occasionally delight a reader of generosity or imagination. It will not satisfy his ideas of what poetry should be, unless his ideas are deplorable ones; but how many poems will? It is important for us to realize that many of the values of good poetry are irreconcilable: if some good poems have a tough reasonableness underneath the slight lyric grace—as the Stagirite says—a great many have a tender unreasonableness. (In the old days I should have suggested borrowing a few nuclear physicists to persuade us that it is possible and profitable to use one set of hypotheses on Monday, Wednesday, and Friday, and another set the rest of the week; but today it would be like borrowing the murderers from *Macbeth*—one could not listen for trembling.) Academic critics will overestimate de la Mare's book because he writes the "right" sort of poetry—that is, romantic and traditional; modernist critics will underestimate it because he writes the "wrong" sort. I should say that he sometimes, rarely, writes poetry that is good of its kind, and that this is the only sort of good poetry there is: there is no kind plainly different from, and plainly superior to, all the rest—though some kind of rough, *ceteris paribus* valuing of the kinds is possible.

De la Mare comes so late in the development of romanticism that, though he still believes in the romantic's world, he believes in it helplessly and hopelessly, as a long and necessarily (though perhaps not "really") lost cause. For its sweet ghost—a spectre that is haunting the industrial and scientific world that has destroyed it—he feels a nostalgic, rapt despair. Restrained by considerations neither of expediency nor of possibility, his romantic doctrines have become extraordinarily characteristic and extravagant: the forlorn hope is always the purest hope. Yet he grieves not so much over what has happened to everybody as over what must necessarily happen to anybody: over Man and the Present and what Is, these terrible crippling actualizations of the Child and the Past and what Might Have Been. This world of potentiality that he loves and needs is the world of the child *as it seems to the grown-up.* What we are is made bearable for him only by his knowledge that we once were potentially—hence, are—everything that we are not; and dreams and myths and tales, everything else that would be except for the fact that it isn't, are a similar consolation. To him the ordinary rational or practical life resembles the mechanical and rationalized routine, the hysterical anesthesia, of the hypnotized subject: what is real lies above (God, Beauty) or beneath (dreams, animals, children) or around (ghosts, all the beings of myth or *Märchen*). It is children and animals and the Heart ("which with a deeper life doth beat/ Than any wherein thought hath part") that participate in Reality: the blinkers of reason confine our conscious, systematic knowledge to what is irrelevant. Yet de la Mare's Heart not only has its reasons but does a surprising amount of reasoning with them, and its sentences are grammatical and full of semi-colons. He does not share the characteristic superstition of much modern opinion: that generalization or "statement" has no place in poetry.

De la Mare's world is neither the best nor the worst but the most enchanted of all possible worlds. It assures us that if reality is not necessarily what we should like it to be, it is necessarily what we feel it to be: to be is to be *felt*. In the "clear grave dark" universe of these poems Falstaff and a ghost are ontologically equal, and both of them are ontologically superior to you, reader, unless you appeal to de la Mare a good deal more than there is any reason to suppose you do. Unfortunately, this criterion is a thoroughly accidental one; if de la Mare happened to develop a taste for science, a whole new category of reality would suddenly come into being. The images he treats everything in terms of, the choir and furniture of his world, demonstrate beyond question what is Real to him; dreams; intuition; emotions, perceptions—any quality or essence known sympathetically and valued intrinsically; the more appealing universals (Beauty or Truth is Real, entropy or triangularity isn't); the supernatural—everything from elves and Ariel to those powers or deities with which the natural world is haunted; nature, especially moonlight, the stars, clouds, trees, the pleasanter and better-known animals, flowers, the sea, and so forth; and children. A child asleep is for de la Mare the archetype of all knowledge: the delicate and secure innocence of the child's face mirrors a knowledge beyond any wisdom, "maps secrets stranger than the seas',/ In hieroglyphics more austere,/ And

older far than Rameses'." (It is odd—but human, all too human
—that this judgment is never extended to puppies or kittens,
which have the same wonderful look.) If we happened to be
oviparous, and our children looked like young owls or robins,
this idea would hardly have occurred to de la Mare. But such an
extension to the universe itself of a principle derived from one
contingent, infinitesimal segment of that universe is too common
for its recognition to involve much blame.

De la Mare uses delicately and sometimes magically the
ordinary vocabulary of the romantic poets ("lorn as curlew's in
the hush/ Of dewfall"); but he has a feeling for terse, homely,
concrete phrasing that is not ordinary, and a surprising Hardyish
willingness to use awkward and ineffective abstractions because he spontaneously thinks of a subject in those terms. He
uses the most flagrantly Poetic diction, half for old-fashioned
manners and half for love: he seems to share the Collegiate
Dictionary's frightening belief that a poem is "a composition
in verse, characterized by imagination and poetic diction."
Similarly he thinks the gaudiest trappings of Elizabethan tragedy intrinsically valuable, and his fervidly romantic and dramatic speeches in blank verse are close to those of Kipling's
mock-Elizabethan play-scenes. (His poems are *about* part of the
pre-1914 world, not our own—though there is something pre-
scient in their gloom.) When he writes in the grand manner it is
with a certain innocence, as children act out an execution; he is
genuinely unassuming, a mouse in a corner, and never thinks to
tell you, as better but vainer poets do: "Now I am going to be
humble."

It is easy to complain that de la Mare writes about unreality;

153

but how *can* anybody write about unreality? From his children and ghosts one learns little about children and nothing about ghosts, but one learns a great deal of the reality of which both his ghosts and his children are projections, of the wishes and lacks and love that have produced their "unreality." (We read religious poems not to learn about God but to learn about men.) At the very least de la Mare is a perspective of reality, a way of sight, that satisfies the limitations he and his readers share, and that exposes to his readers the limitations that are peculiar to de la Mare—or to themselves. He has made himself a fool for the sake of Faerie, for the sake of everything that is irrational, impractical, and at the same time essential; and because he has persisted in his folly his best poems—limited and extravagant as they are—are full of the personal distinction, the involuntary individuality that are marks of a real poet. But his poetry represents our world only as the flickering shade-pattern of leaves upon an arm can represent the arm; the hard hot flesh in the sunlight has nothing to stand for it but vacancy.

II.

ALTHOUGH the first part of Alex Comfort's novel, *The Power House*, is better than anything in *The Song of Lazarus*, he is potentially and in diffusion a fairly interesting poet. Unfortunately, neither organization nor economy is natural to him, and the extensive, rather clumsy energy of his prose is tenuous in his verse. One out of a dozen of his phrases is successful; the other eleven are typical—typical enough to tell you how old he is, where he lives, whom he reads. (Appropriation is the sincerest flattery, as you can see when workers take over the state, or when Mr. Comfort infringes again and again on such notorious patents as Dylan Thomas's "candle in the thighs.") In their elegiac, almost pastoral reflection in these poems, death and the War seem hardly more than allegorical emanations of some passive, amoral reality. There flows by interminably a clear, ripe, shining, well-watered, rather French and feminine nature: blood or vague sexual fluids pulse through its imagined vessels, and as you wander over the "chalk-pit's navel" or the "fruitful thighs of the corn," you feel that you are in some modernist room where the woods are blond, the hues unsaturated, and the designs unarresting but full of symbols borrowed from *The Interpretation of Dreams*. But the inhabitants of this room are dead or dying; everywhere you stumble there are the bones (improbably polished bones, but bones) that the wars of bad men in far-off capitals have scattered here. This pleasant enough osseous nonsense—the all too articulate skeletons popping, like jack-in-the-boxes, from the duped and temporary flesh—makes it hard to take any death seriously, or to remember that Mr. Comfort is talking about the deaths, not of Corydon and last fall's leaves, but of the peoples of the Second World War.

Mr. Comfort was a conscientious objector; so it is unnecessary to say that he has both courage and individual judgment. But the good luck that made him an interne in a London hospital instead of a laborer in some concentration camp in the country has cut him off from all of us in his poems: he is the isolated, pacifist, individualistic anarchist who tells the truth about things to the deceived homogeneous mass that is everybody else. This truth has the attractive and improbable simplicity of one of those Robinson Crusoe demonstrations that the Jevonian economist used to specialize in. Mr. Comfort believes in conscientious disobedience: if no one obeys the government there will be no war. There can be war only because people are dupes—"upright clock-faced citizens" who are fooled by the "loaded dice," the "stacked cards" of the "drunkards and whoremasters" who are their governors. The poet's irritation at the stupidity of the corpses weakens his pastoral and generalized grief for them; besides, these are the wholesale deaths that happen to other people, not the petty retail deaths that happen to you and yours. And he never wonders: how does it feel to be a dupe?

But it is the way things are for us—not the way they would be if we were rational, economic, Benthamic men, intelligently determining the algebraic sum of our own interests—that has to matter to that witness of the actions of men, the poet. Between Mr. Comfort and the soldiers there is a final barrier: he is right and they are wrong; and he cannot share the sympathetic, unwilling identity in which all their differences are buried—their uneasy knowledge that the mechanics of their living and someone else's dying is statistical. It is hard for him to feel for one of them an unmixed sorrow, since he can't help thinking, "He'd have been all right if he'd only had sense enough to disobey." But he means, *if they'd only all had sense enough to disobey:* though he seems to think he is making plausible political proposals, he is actually making impossible moral demands. To him, as he states in an essay, any resistance to any state is an intrinsic good—since all states are equally and absolutely evil; a person is necessarily virtuous, a citizen necessarily vicious. This is an anarchism possible to the docile inhabitants of a long-established, well-regimented community: that is, to citizens who are protected from each other thoroughly enough, and unnecessarily enough, to believe that there is nothing they need be protected from except the state.

We can hardly fail either to sympathize with Mr. Comfort or to realize that he is right in considering that the states themselves are at present the main danger their citizens face; I do not know whether it would be right for him to sympathize more with us, but—so long as we are his subject matter—it would certainly be expedient. One longs to quote to him Cromwell's "I beseech you, in the bowels of Christ, consider that ye may be mistaken." His version of the unarmed, eventually triumphant proletariat of the anarchists reminds one of its contrary, the armed triumphant proletariat of Marx: I remembered the murals in Mexican market-places of the '30's, with their workers who wave red banners Against the Next Imperialist War—workers whose broad stern faces are complicated by no premonition of their own official future in that war. Yet when one considers the mechanisms of the contemporary states—from the advertising agencies that turn out their principles to the munitions factories that turn out their practice—it is hard to think of the triumph of any proletariat as more than a wistful compensating dream: it is we who wither away, not the state.

III.

TRISTAN CORBIÈRE was born a hundred years ago and died seventy years ago; I heard of no celebration of his centenary, I know almost no one who reads him; but there are not many men who have written poems as good as his, and he can wait in mocking confidence for the world to make its way to his grave. There have been plenty of stray pilgrims: Laforgue, Pound, Eliot, Winters; and this new selection of a few of his poems, along with translations by Walter McElroy, may interest readers in Winters' conclusion about him—that his greatest poems "are probably superior to any French verse of the 19th century save the best of Baudelaire." Certainly no poet of half his greatness is so undervalued and unread.

Mr. McElroy has made a good selection from the poems, though it is sad to see the *Rondels pour après* left out entirely. His translations show a real affection for Corbière, and contain some successful or thoughtful lines or phrases; but a dictionary and the most indifferent French are enough to demonstrate that they have many errors and additions, and a creative irresponsibility, some of the time, to Corbière's exact tone and meaning. Corbière is an extremely hard job for any translator, as his rhetoric depends to an unusual degree on antitheses, puns and half-puns, idioms, clichés, slang, paradoxes: often there is no equivalent word or phrase in English. How are you to translate *viveur vécu?* Spent spend-thrift, wasted wastrel, played-out playboy? These keep most of the form and half of the content, but the heart is gone.

Mr. McElroy decided to rhyme his translations, and he has a complaisance toward rhymes that beats anything that I, a liberal enough rhymer, have ever imagined: he will turn that line of lines, *Tu sais: j'avais lâché la Vie avec des gants*, into *Letting go of life, you know, I wore gloves: those I kept*—in order to have *kept* rhyme with *best*! (This line of Corbière's certainly does temper one's feelings for *I have measured out my life with coffee-spoons;* "Prufrock" and "Gerontion" belong to a genre that a contemporary of General Grant's invented, one understands after reading "Le Poete contumace.") *Calme plat* means *dead calm*, is translated *calm expanse; de travers* becomes—this is not misunderstanding but sheer disregard—*with stately tread; Oui, j'ai beau me palper* becomes *I do well to pinch myself; Tu voulais voir à mon front* becomes *You saw reflected in my face;* and so on. And the translator has an unaccountable habit of missing or disregarding Corbière's jokes: after smiling at *Un barbet qui dormait sous le nom de Fidèle*, one finds that the fairies have left in its place *this* sad bump on a log: *A water-spaniel fond of sleeping, named Trusty*. Later, *Nous nous mettrons au vert du paradis perdu* becomes *We'll find our way to the green of the lost paradise*— but Corbière has said something far better, since *mettre des chevaux au vert* is an idiom meaning *to put horses out to graze*.

Pound called Corbière the most touching of poets—the *Rondels pour après* make his remark seem as truthful as it is unexpected—and Laforgue said, with wistful love, that Corbière's poems are *strident and unwearying as the cry of the sea-gulls:* "We others are all *poetic* . . . He is of a different mettle: an unseizable smoke-dried corsair, bold in his raids." Corbière's range is bewildering: some of his lines, in their short finality, might have been extracted from the *Sayings of Spartans*, but there are plenty of other lines that would make S. J. Perelman envious, consumately reckless rhetorical passages in which the poet's mocking consciousness of what he is doing is half their effect on the reader. "Cris d'aveugles" is full of an agony you have to go to the "terrible sonnets" to match; it would be hard to match precisely the disgust and contempt and identifying acceptance of "Femme"; the neurotic self-dramatizing self-analysis of some of the dramatic monologues is quite as good as anything of the sort in Eliot—whom Corbière of course influenced, though mainly through Laforgue; and there are half the things in the world in "La Rapsode foraine" and "Le Poete contumace," one is willing to swear while one is overcome with them. There are all sorts of things wrong with Corbière, too; but people have talked about his faults (or not mentioned them because they never mentioned him) for almost a hundred years now—it is time to talk for a hundred years about his virtues.

The poems have a rude, laconic strength, a hammering and reckless wit, that work themselves up (with an ingenuity that would shame any Devil) into the blankest or most sardonic exaggeration; here is Paris by sheet lightning:

> *La: vivre à coups de fouet!—passer*
> *En fiacre, en correctionelle;*
> *Repasser à la ritournelle,*
> *Se dépasser, et trépasser!* . . .

The bad and mediocre poems in *Les Amours jaunes* are a deliberate and repeated slap in the face of things—poems that tell you the worst about themselves, and anything else that comes to hand, almost as a principle of composition. (Raleigh's "The Lie" is an accidental prototype, both in content and form, of one or two of these.) Their antagonistic, obstinate, and monotonous wit here and there breaks out into one of those open jeers that people always notice in Villon: for instance, the epigraph of *Rapsodie du sourd* is: "*Le silence est d'or.—Saint Jean Chrysostome.*" One section of *Les Amours jaunes* is called *Raccrocs*— Flukes—and one word could hardly sum up better the whole sardonic side of Corbière: if the ball climbs the chandelier, with *this* player it is no fluke. Beethoven is supposed to have improvised until a whole drawing-room wept, and then to have laughed at them—half mockingly, half sympathetically, and altogether out of the consciousness of power; this consciousness of power is never absent from Corbière, who always answers our bewilderment with the same *Surprise is my profession.* The prevailing irony that blows through his poems is neither Byronic nor Laforguian, but something far more complicated, since it does not replace an idealistic or sentimental attitude with a "disillusioned" one, but mocks at part of each and accepts part of each; and the mockery and the acceptance are fused, sometimes, in one incandescent phrase—are transfigured, sometimes, by a cruel and magical tenderness:

> *Dors: ce lit est le tien . . . Tu n'iras plus au nôtre.*
> *—Qui dort dîne.—A tes dents viendra tout seul le foin.*
> *Dors: on t'aimera bien—L'aime c'est toujours l'Autre . . .*
> *Rêve: La plus aimée est toujours la plus loin . . .*
>
> *Dors: on t'appellera beau décrocheur d'etoiles!*
> *Chevacheur de rayons! . . . quand il fera bien noir;*

Et l'ange du plafond, maigre araignée, au soir,
—Espoir—sur ton front vide ira filer ses toiles.

Museleur de voilette! un baiser sous le voile
T'attend . . . on ne sait où; ferme les yeux pour voir.
Ris: les premiers honneurs t'attendent sous le poêle.

On cassera ton nez d'un bon coup d'encensoir,
Doux fumet! pour la trogne en fleur, pleine de moelle
D'un sacristain très bien, avec son éteignoir.

Corbière is far too serious a poet to be solemn; what he says he means; but he says it in a series of astonishingly colloquial and idiomatic exclamations—his speech, often, is a sort of living contradiction. Puns, mocking half-dead metaphors, parodied clichés, antitheses and paradoxes, idioms exploited on every level, are the seven-league crutches on which the poems bound wildly forward. If nature, once, made no jumps, it was different from Corbière, who progresses by nothing else; one of his poems passes through its aggregation of exclamations, interjections, vocatives, imperatives as an electron passes through its orbits—now here, now there, and in between nowhere.

There is no one else as close to Villon: at his rare best Corbière does equal justice both to what we want and what we get, and his wonderful toughness and irony and intelligence come through a conclusive realization of emotion and spirit, not through any escape from either. Corbière's own epitaph ends:

Il mourut en s'attendant vivre
Et vécu s'attendant mourir.

He lived and died catercornered, *de travers*—obsessed not just by the hard way but by the hardest way: he is a rock set against all the currents of the world.

IV.

MURIEL RUKEYSER is a forcible writer with a considerable talent for emotional rhetoric; but she works with a random melodramatic hand, and with rather unfortunate models and standards. One feels about most of her poems almost as one feels about the girl on last year's calendar, and prefers to think of Miss Rukeyser only as the poet who wrote "Ajanta." There is nothing so successful as "Ajanta" in her new book, *The Green Wave;* the best poem in the book, I think, is "Mrs. Walpurga," a sliding, oil-and-honey, easily sexual fantasy, half dream, half nightmare.

It is hard not to feel indifferent toward any particular poem in *The Green Wave*, since you can see that Miss Rukeyser—and not just Miss Rukeyser—could turn out a thousand more quite like it. The poems are, essentially, improvisations, easy reworkings of the automatic images of a rhetorical-emotional trance-state in which everything slides into everything else, in which everything is no more than the transition to everything else: if my reader will get as woolly-headed and as oracularly emotional as he can—as if, say, he were listening to *Tristan* with complete sympathy and empathy—and then utter, in a slow wavy voice, joined by *ands*, the most powerful and troubling images he can think of on the spur of the moment, he will get the raw material of one of Miss Rukeyser's elegies, of George Barker's elegies, of many other contemporary poems. But where everything is a dream, dreams are nothing: after a whole book of images changing into images, the reader would trade tons of them for one scruple of common logic, one everyday unchanging fact, one line as blessedly prosaic as

> *A Mr. Wilkinson, a clergyman.*

After all, Proust's "fork, fork, Francis Jammes" dream has so much effect precisely because Norpois has never uttered a dreaming word. But many poets—I'm not talking about Miss Rukeyser now—write as if they had been decerebrated, and not simply lobotomized, as a cure for their melancholia.

Consider this more than typical quotation:

> *Man, an explosion walking through the night in*
> *Rich and intolerable loneliness.*
> *Cathedrals writhing gold against their clouds*
> *And a child asking the fiery pure questions.*

Such a passage is by no means unsuccessful. *An explosion walking* has only the sort of effectiveness that *Did you ever see a dream walking?* has, but it is effective; the opposition of *rich* and *intolerable*, of *rich* and *loneliness*, gives the whole phrase a contradictory verisimilitude of a somewhat obvious kind; *writhing gold* is almost exactly accurate for such a Mexican cathedral as Miss Rukeyser is describing, though it has the disadvantage of sounding like general rhetoric; the *their* in the phrase *their clouds* not only has an enlivening, personifying effect, but also gives some-

thing of the personal possession of its ground that an overwhelming figure often seems to have. And yet this whole passage is not
much more than a half-particularized sugar-coating for a feeling
that is itself not much more than general rhetoric; there is something adulterated, attitudinizing, merely conventional, about
both the expression of her attitude and the attitude. Here, just as
it usually is, Miss Rukeyser's real concern is to tell the reader,
as excitingly as she can, how he ought to feel about something.
She barely pretends to show him the thing and let him feel for
himself; her rhetoric is an oratorical, oracular testimonial designed to make him buy it without even looking. *Are* the questions pure and fiery? Always, in such poetry as this. The rhythm
of every last word is crying: "Don't ask questions—lie back,
child! Don't you want to be moved?" Yes; but more than this,
and more specifically than this. Tell us the questions and we can
see whether they're pure and fiery. And—and it's all so familiar
. . . Miss Rukeyser almost asks us to be unjust to her, to treat
her as an orator, not a poet, and to quote to her Kant's crushing
paragraphs (in the *Critique of Judgment*) about the difference
between oratory and poetry.

Miss Rukeyser's worst and most commonplace lines—there
aren't too many—are all rhetorical sublimations of the horrible
advertising-agency idealism of Corwin or Fast or MacLeish or
the National Association of Manufacturers, of sermons and
radio programs and editorials and speeches: what our ignorant
forbears called *cant*. But Miss Rukeyser is sometimes so original
—if one leaves a few comic-strips out of the question—in her use
of a sexual or Freudian imagery for this idealism that one
feels, with dismay and delight, that one is listening to the

Common Woman of our century, a siren photographed in a sequin bathing-suit, on rocks like boiled potatoes, for the week-end edition of *PM*, in order to bring sex to the deserving poor. When you think of yourself as that terrible thing, a public figure—and Miss Rukeyser does to some extent—it is hard to decide exactly what you do feel, what the real reasons are; and how are the images and emotions of Miss Rukeyser's dream-rhetoric going to decide between *do* and *should*, *real* and *good?* The average poem in *The Green Wave* is all flesh and feeling and fantasy: as if reality were a pure blooming buzz, with the poet murmuring to the poem, "Flow, flow!" Yet all the time the poem keeps repeating, keeps remembering to repeat, that it is a *good* girl—that it is, after all, dying for the people; the reader trudges, full of uneasy delight, through the labyrinthine corridors of this strange, moral, sexual wish-fantasy for which he is to be awarded, somehow, a gold star by the Perfect State.

V.

THE MOST SUCCESSFUL of R. P. Blackmur's early poems were modeled on those of Yeats. Their style was at once too open and too objective for the material and temperament of the poet— and such an inheritance has to be worked out, not simply appropriated, if it is ever to be your own. Many of Mr. Blackmur's later poems were written as the man in the story played the violin, by main force; they seemed interesting as an awkward, tortured, and honest diary, but surprisingly unsuccessful as works of art. One felt that they were mired both in their raw material and—more especially—in the raw act of writing, of making: they had too little spontaneity, grace, or autonomy to give delight. But two or three of the poems in this last book, *The Good European*, are successful, and most of them are interesting. They are written in a style that is partly an extension of the night side of Hopkins, partly a sort of lowest common denominator of "the" traditional English poetic style, and partly no style at all, speech whose extraordinary awkwardness or strain is a guarantee of truth or the intention of truth.

These are poems of the most extreme situations possible, of a constricted, turned-in-upon-itself, contorted, almost tetanic agony: the poet not only works against the grain of things, but the grain is all knots. Sometimes the poems rise into one of Hopkins's gasps of kinaesthetic ecstasy: "wild waste winnowing." But usually they are trapped in the middles, not the endings, of the "terrible sonnets," or in the even more terrible middles-without-end of the unfinished poems, or—most of all— in the letters: in Hopkins's isolated capitalized sentence "BUT WHAT DOES ANYTHING AT ALL MATTER?" The "winch" from which Hopkins's skylark unwound its song has changed into the rabbit's "small ear-flattened, brown, zig-zagging anguished winch of sound," as the crow kills it. Sometimes this is pure pain, not art at all, and one is sharing in the nightmare of a man sitting in the midst of his own entrails, knitting them all night into the tapestry which he unknits all day. But there is even in these poems little of that horrible relishing complacency with which so many existential thinkers insist upon the worst; the poems try desperately for any way out, either for the Comforter—*some* sort of comforter—or else for that coldest comfort, understanding. Some of the most successful poems have quasi-theological "happy endings" in which there emerges from the machine not God but the Name of God, the "necessary, up-welling swaddling cry" of hope. (Compare the endings of *The Three Sisters, Uncle Vanya,* and *Gusev.*) But the main subject of the poems is evil: evil as such, a real and final evil; so they are not Christian poems at all. Real evil surely is what is arbitrarily *so* in the universe, all that is undeserved and irremediable; for Christianity evil is inherent neither in God nor in the universe, but springs full-armed, unexplained and unexplainable, from the Fall (of Satan and of man); and so long as *we* are to blame for evil, so long as God is free from it—free to save us from that evil which we are and have deserved to be—real evil, final evil, does not exist. It is interestingly grotesque that some Christians should be as fond as they are of condemning all "secular thinkers" for their disregard of evil. Perhaps the Buddhists should have sent more missionaries to the West.

Mr. Blackmur's poems are troubling, difficult, and serious poems; one needs a good deal of time to get used to them—and they are printed, quite elaborately, in an extraordinary type that one has almost to learn to read. Readers are most likely to be repelled by their stubborn awkwardness; their crudities, their sometimes barbarous word-twisting; their nightmarish unpleas-antness; their echoes. But one could defend them by saying that the awkwardness is that persisted-in folly which becomes wis-dom; that the crudities ruin some poems and flaw others, but in the two or three best poems disappear or are incidental; that the nightmarishness is also that of our world; and that the echoes are either inconsequential (like the variations, on page eighteen, on the Epitaph of another stray, still-born philosopher) or else the consequence of using Hopkins as a source pretty much as the metaphysicals used Donne ("The Light Left On" is a clear, almost slavish example). The poems do not lend themselves to quotation, but I will quote the end of a poem which will surely move anyone, "The Rape of Europa":

> *. . . The muck she lies in mocks the muck of birth,*
> *and what is born lies blameless in her lap.*
>
> *Horror got out of horror may yet be blest*
> *when the great scar of birth begins to scab*
> *and with each change of weather pull and burn*
> *and the wound verge on flow. What bore, tore;*
> *the horror and the glory are the same.*
> *Man's hope the wound, God's memory the scar!*
> *—else what is born lies nameless in her lap.*

A passage like this is not the work of what people call a born poet: some awkwardness or lameness persists under the surface of the verse, or emerges in rhythms like "and with each change of weather pull and burn/ and the wound verge on flow"; the terms in which the passage is conceived are embarrassingly strained and literal, and its language is self-conscious—for instance, one line is derived from a sentence of Eliot's that seems to haunt Mr. Blackmur; and nothing in the passage has the felicity or finality one expects from the finest verse. But when you have said these things you have still not said something more important: that the passage is the work of an intelligent, pitying, and serious imagination.

VI.

THIS IS so much the age of anthologies that it is surprising that poets still waste their time on books of verse, instead of writing anthologies in the first place. If you are about to print a book of poems, don't: make up a few names and biographical sketches with which to punctuate your manuscript, change its title to *Poems of Democracy*, and you will find yourself transformed from an old pumpkin, always in the red, to a shiny black new coach. For the average reader knows poetry mainly from anthologies, just as he knows philosophy mainly from histories of philosophy or textbooks: the *Complete Someone*—hundreds or thousands of small-type, double-column pages of *poetry*, without one informing repentant sentence of ordinary prose—evokes from him a start of that savage and unreasoning timidity, that *horror vacui*, with which he stares at the lemmas and corollaries of Spinoza's *Ethics*. Those cultural entrepreneurs, the anthologists, have become figures of melancholy and deciding importance for the average reader of poetry, a man of great scope and little grasp, who still knows what he likes—in the anthologies.

And yet if you ask, "What do I need to become an anthologist?" it is difficult to answer, as one would like to: "Taste." Zeal and a publisher seem the irreducible and, usually, unexceeded minimum. The typical anthologist is a sort of Gallup

Poll with connections—often astonishing ones; it is hard to know whether he is printing a poem because he likes it, because his acquaintances tell him he ought to, or because he went to high school with the poet. But certainly he is beyond good or evil, and stares over his herds of poets like a patriarch, nodding or pointing with a large industrial air.

Anthologies are, ideally, an essential species of criticism. Nothing expresses and exposes your taste so completely—nothing is your taste so nearly—as that vague final treasury of the *really* best poems that grows in your head all your life, and that finds ambiguous and expedient utterance, if you are an anthologist, in the more "objective" anthology you send your publishers. Your readers will have to infer that taste mainly from the more unusual inclusions and omissions of your anthology. (You may leave out James Whitcomb Riley because you are afraid of being laughed at, but if you leave out Spenser you mean business.) It is a pity that Arnold's touchstones, which as they are remind one of the charm bracelets little girls wear, never evolved into an anthology. Nobody quotes so well as Eliot—his quotations and preferences have helped to generate two of the better modern anthologies, those of Charles Williams and Michael Roberts; it is a great pity that he has never made an anthology of his own. Even a highly idiosyncratic and biased taste can produce charming or valuable anthologies of a more personal sort: imagine the *Moral Treasury* of Yvor Winters! And since anthologies are a part of criticism, there should be anthologies which explain instead of evaluating: which demonstrate, say, the rise and fall of a certain way of looking at the world, by reproducing its most typical, influential, or exaggerated expressions, not merely its most poetically successful ones. But I am talking about unusual or non-existent anthologies, not the commercial conveniences one ordinarily encounters in bookstores.

Stanton A. Coblentz's anthology, *The Music Makers*, is not so much a commercial convenience as a crusade. Any poem must be (1) singing, (2) magical, (3) easy to understand: this is a (very) synthetic a priori judgment of Mr. Coblentz's, and by a sufficiently unreflecting use of it he is able to condemn the Benéts as modernist poets, and to compile an anthology of "traditional" contemporary poems that is the most nearly conclusive—and the most awingly dreary—justification of modernist poetry that has ever been devised. These poems are the imitation not of nature but of Poems, and at their worst they make Frederick the Great's adaptations of Voltaire seem *res gestae*.

A Little Treasury of Modern Poetry is a standard Oscar Williams production: a preface which is sometimes ordinary sense, and sometimes a Cry from the Heart of the Poet ("Now I like high and serious poetry to such a degree that I cannot imagine life worth living without it . . . Since with God all things are possible, poets and readers in unison may work their own miracle by which the human heart may yet so enlarge that it outweighs the atomic bomb"); oval Portraits of the Poets; a dust-jacket that crams down the gullets of the hungry sheep this "authoritative collection of the best poems written during the last fifty years," and that ends, as always, with the truthful statement that W. H. Auden prefers the poetry of Oscar Williams to that of Wallace Stevens and Dylan Thomas. (At

172

this point I always wish that the grasses were waving over me and over Auden too.) After looking unbelievingly at "The Great Lover" and "The Man with the Hoe" and "I Have a Rendezvous with Death" and "Chimborazo, Cotapaxi" and "They Went Forth to Battle but They Always Fell"; after reading poems by Ben Maddow, Helen Hoyt, Frederick Mortimer Clapp, Edith Wyatt, Esther Mathews, and many another; after looking in vain for a single poem by Robert Lowell, Sturge Moore, Henry Reed, Howard Baker, and many another; after finding in the Light Verse section Yeats's wonderful and heartbreaking "John Kinsella's Lament for Mrs. Mary Moore"; after working a way through excessive wastes of Barker and Fuller and Manifold and Masefield and Symons and Prokosch and Derwood and Wylie and Teasdale and Treece and John Hall Wheelock; after noticing what an extremely poor job of selection Mr. Williams has done with Auden, Bridges, Hardy, Housman, Pound, MacNeice, Graves, Moore, and others—after all this, the reader may feel like damning Mr. Williams and his works without one further thought. But he shouldn't; Mr. Williams is, I think, one of the best of this crew of professional anthologists, and his anthology has plenty of good things to go along with the bad: great quantities of Hopkins, Yeats, Eliot, Dylan Thomas, Auden, Tate, Frost, and other fine poets; some, though not enough, Empson and Marianne Moore and Elizabeth Bishop and William Carlos Williams; and seldom-anthologized poems like "Missing Dates," "Roosters," "Song for the Clatter-Bones," "Scyros," "John Kinsella's Lament," and several others. (Also, the book has the merit of containing a considerably larger selection of Oscar Williams's poems than I have ever seen in any other anthology. There are nine of his poems—and five of Hardy's. It takes a lot of courage to like your own poetry almost twice as well as Hardy's.)

Mr. Williams is clever enough to print many of those poems that have become limitedly famous among intelligent readers and critics; and in spite of the mass of bad poetry that weighs it down, his anthology gives a forcible impression of all the good poetry that has been written in the last fifty or sixty years. Mr. Williams has a real taste for good poetry; that he has just as real a taste for bad, spoils his book. He has a soft spot in his heart—a softer spot, I mean—for any young English or English-educated or English-influenced poet who gushes, and as a result his Treasury is haunted by a flock of maundering harpies who insist on giving you a pound of their heart's blood with any random ounce of sense.

I am grateful to Richard Eberhart and Selden Rodman, the editors of *War and the Poet*, for two enchanting poems entirely new to me. One, "The Maunding Soldier, or the Fruits of Warre Is Beggary," is a Falstaffian ballad of extraordinary humor and command; the other is the poem—the only poem, woe's me—of a predecessor of Dante's named Niccolo degli Albizzi. I wish that he had written as many poems as Southey. Who could forget the "black yellow smoke-dried visages" of his defeated, starving, and shamefaced troops, "stumbling for hunger on their marrow-bones/ Like barrels rolling, jolting . . . their eyes, like hanged men's, turning the wrong way"? He is the only poet I know who could have written "Johnny, I Hardly Knew Ye," for he ends his poem:

Their arms all gone, not even their swords are saved;
And each as silent as a man being shaved.

Otherwise *War and the Poet* is not much. It is thoroughly topical in conception, though it appears, like the P-80, a little late for combat. Its editors have great enthusiasm, moderate sensibility, and little judgment. After reading prefaces that are gushing and eccentric, notes that are random and gossipy, and war poems that are sometimes good, sometimes bad, and sometimes not war poems at all, you know a great deal about the emotions and ideals of the editors, but you have no idea whether either of them can tell a good poem from a bad. Some of their judgments are hardly normative at all: only chance or necessity could have led them to include obviously bad or mediocre poems by Shaemas O'Sheel or Don Gordon or Kenneth Patchen or Timothy Corsellis or Harry Brown or such, while they were leaving out "Nineteen Hundred and Nineteen" and Yeats's other poems about the Irish revolution; "Willie MacIntosh"; Owens's "Exposure"; Melville's best war poems; Tate's poem about the dead of the Civil War; and many, many more. Often they pick the right poet but the wrong poem: imagine representing Yeats by nothing but "An Irish Airman Foresees His Death"! Imagine choosing from the Bible neither the 137th Psalm nor that chorus of wondering exultation over fallen Assyria that begins, "Hell from beneath is moved for thee to meet thee at thy coming," and that goes on, "How art thou fallen from Heaven, O Lucifer, son of the morning!" There are good poems in the anthology, but far too few to leaven a lump of its size.

But there is one thing in *War and the Poet* that deserves to be immortal. Its dust-jacket, after condemning politicians, scientists, journalists, and "literary pundits" for their parts in the war, concludes: "Only the poets, inspired by a tradition of humanism that brooked no barriers of race or creed, kept faith." Surely this is the most charitable conclusion that anyone anywhere has ever come to.

VII.

SOMETIMES it is hard to criticize, one wants only to chronicle. The good and mediocre books come in from week to week, and I put them aside and read them and think of what to say; but the "worthless" books come in day after day, like the cries and truck sounds from the street, and there is nothing that anyone could think of that is good enough for them. In the bad type of the thin pamphlets, in hand-set lines on imported paper, people's hard lives and hopeless ambitions have expressed themselves more directly and heartbreakingly than they have ever been expressed in any work of art: it is as if the writers had sent you their ripped-out arms and legs, with "This is a poem" scrawled on them in lipstick. After a while one is embarrassed not so much for them as for poetry, which is for these poor poets one more of the openings against which everyone in the end beats his brains out; and one finds it unbearable that poetry should be so hard to write—a game of Pin the Tail on the Donkey in

176

which there is for most of the players no tail, no donkey, not
even a booby prize. If there were only some mechanism (like
Seurat's proposed system of painting, or the projected Universal
Algebra that Gödel believes Leibnitz to have perfected and mis-
laid) for reasonably and systematically converting into poetry
what we see and feel and are! When one reads the verse of
people who cannot write poems—people who sometimes have
more intelligence, sensibility, and moral discrimination than
most of the poets—it is hard not to regard the Muse as a sort of
fairy godmother who says to the poet, after her colleagues have
showered on him the most disconcerting and ambiguous gifts,
"Well, never mind. You're still the only one that can write
poetry."

It seems a detestable joke that the "national poet of the
Ukraine"—kept a private in the army for ten years, and for-
bidden by the Czar to read, to draw, or even to write a letter—
should not have for his pain one decent poem. A poor Air Corps
sergeant spends two and a half years on Attu and Kiska, and at
the end of the time his verse about the war is indistinguishable
from Browder's brother's parrot's. How cruel that a cardinal—
for one of these books is a cardinal's—should write verses worse
than his youngest choir-boy's! But in this universe of bad poetry
everyone is compelled by the decrees of an unarguable Necessity
to murder his mother and marry his father, to turn somersaults
widdershins around his own funeral, to do everything that his
worst and most imaginative enemy could wish. It would be a
hard heart and a dull head that could condemn, except with a
sort of sacred awe, such poets for anything that they have done

—or rather, for anything that has been done to them: for they have never *made* anything, they have suffered their poetry as helplessly as they have anything else; so that it is neither the imitation of life nor a slice of life but life itself—beyond good, beyond evil, and certainly beyond reviewing.

The Humble Animal

I HAVE read Marianne Moore's poetry too many years and too many times not to be afraid that both the poems and my feelings about them will be poorly represented by anything I write. It might be better to say, like Graves's Augustus, "Words fail me, my lords," and to go through *What Are Years* pointing. This is Miss Moore's own method of criticism, as anyone who has read one of her reviews will remember; it would be a rude kind of justice to make a criticism of her poetry quotations and a few conjunctions.

One critic has said that Miss Moore's poetry is not poetry at all, but criticism—actually even her criticism is not criticism but an inferior sort of poetry. She not only can, but must, make poetry out of everything and anything: she is like Midas, or like Mozart choosing unpromising themes for the fun of it, or like one of those princesses whom wizards force to manufacture sheets out of nettles. And yet there is one thing Miss Moore has a distaste for making poetry of: the Poetic. She has made a principle out of refusing to believe that there is any such thing as the antipoetic; her poems restore to poetry the "business documents and school books" that Tolstoy took away.

Pound wrote one famous sentence of advice which—to judge from the practice of most of the poets who read it—was understood as: *Poetry must be just as badly written as prose.* Miss Moore understood it more as it was meant to be understood: her poetry, not satisfied with the difficulties of verse, has added to them those of prose. Her poems have the virtues—form, concentration, emotion, observation, imagination, and so on—that one expects of poetry; but one also finds in them, in supersaturated solution, some of the virtues of good prose. Miss Moore's language fits Wordsworth's formula for the language of poetry surprisingly well—something that will disquiet lovers of either of the two poets, though not lovers of both; but I am sure Wordsworth would have looked at it with uncomfortable dislike, and have called it the language of extraordinary women. This would be true: Miss Moore, in spite of a restraint unparalleled in our time, is a natural, excessive, and magnificent eccentric. (On a small scale, of course; like all cultivated Americans, she is afraid of size.) Eccentricity has been to her a first resort, an easy but inescapable refuge.

Miss Moore's forms have the lacy, mathematical extravagance of snowflakes, seem as arbitrary as the prohibitions in fairy tales; but they work as those work—disregard them and everything goes to pieces. Her forms, tricks and all, are like the aria of the Queen of the Night: the intricate and artificial elaboration not only does not conflict with the emotion but is its vehicle. And her machinery—bestiary, rather—fits both the form and final content of her poems as precisely as if all three were pieces of some extraordinary puzzle. Another of the finest American poets, Wallace Stevens, is as addicted to exotic properties; but his often get in the way of what he has to say, or hide from him the fact that he does not, this time, care to say anything much. The things *are* what Miss Moore wants to say, and express her as naturally and satisfactorily as the Lamb and the Tyger did God. (Some true wit—Miss Moore, I suppose—put an index at the back of *Observations*, the early collection of her poems.) A style ought to make it easy for you to say all that you have to say, not, as most do, make it impossible for you to get free from one narrowed range of experience and expression; Miss Moore's style, whether it seems to or not, does the first—this is proved by the fact that her poetry is richer, more balanced, and more objective than her prose. Nobody else's mechanism and mannerisms come so close to being independently satisfactory— like the Cheshire Cat's smile, which bewitched one for some time after the cat was gone. (Sometimes the smile is almost better than the cat: I once read, in a college newspaper's account of a lecture, that poets put "real toes in imaginary gardens, as Mary Ann Moore says.")

It would be stupid not to see Miss Moore in all her protective creatures—"another armored animal," she once reflects, or confesses. Patience, honesty, the courage that is never conscious of itself because it has always taken itself for granted— all the qualities she distils from, or infuses into, the real pastoral of natural history books, she is at last able to permit even to man, looking at him (in the beautiful "The Pangolin") as equably, carefully, and affectionately as she ever looked at any animal. "The Pangolin" may be her best poem; it is certainly one of the most moving, honest, and haunting poems that anyone has written in our century.

Miss Moore realizes that there is no such thing as the *Ding an Sich*, that the relations *are* the thing; that the outside, looked at hard enough, is the inside; that the wrinkles are only the erosion of habitual emotion. She shows that everything is related to everything else, by comparing everything to everything else; no one has compared successfully more disparate objects. She has as careful and acute an eye as anybody alive, and almost as good a tongue: so that when she describes something, a carrot, it is as if she had taken the carrot's cries in some final crisis, cries that hold in themselves a whole mode of existence. One finds in her poems so much wit and particularity and observation; a knowledge of "prosaic" words that reminds one of *Comus;* a texture that will withstand any amount of rereading; a restraint and delicacy that make many more powerful poems seem obvious. And, over and above the love and care and knowledge she has lavished on the smallest details of the poems, Miss Moore is an oddly moral writer, one who coalesces moralities hardly ever found together; she is even, extraordinarily enough in our time, a writer with a happy ending—of a kind.

One could make a queer economic-historical analysis of Miss Moore, as the representative of a morality divorced both from religion and from economics, of a class-segment that has almost been freed either from power or from guilt—whose cultivation, because of its helplessness and poverty, is touching. One might say that Miss Moore is, fragmentarily, Henry James in pure crystalline form. (Sometimes James's morality, in its last extrav-

agance, is one more Great Game, a species of ethical hydro-
ponics.) In Miss Moore's poems religion and economics are
ghosts. Clergymen are spare cultivated old men, friends of your
father, living scrupulously off dwindling incomes, who on the
lawn tell you occasionally, not without a dry and absent im-
pressiveness, about unfrequented hallways of the Old Testament. Business, the West, furnish you with no more than an
odd quotation about the paper of an encyclopedia, and in the
colonies of the West there are neither workers nor hunger, only
pandas. Society is the incredible monster you inhabit, like the
whale in Lucian; for many years, long before your birth even,
there has been nothing anyone could do—so while you wait
under the shade of that great doom you do well and, whether
any bless you or not, are blessed. Alone in your civility, precariously safe and beautiful in the enforced essential privacy
of late individualism, you are like the reed which escapes, perhaps, the storm that wrecks the forest; or like the humble, the
children and sparrows, who served as models for salvation in the
similar convulsions of an earlier world. And what an advantage
it is to be poor and humble, to have lost your stake in the game
that corrupts even if you play unwillingly and without belief!
It is you who can sit still—no need to wish to—and keep your
mouth shut, or speak so softly and dryly it is as good as silence.

Miss Moore has great limitations—her work is one long
triumph of them; but it was sad, for so many years, to see them
and nothing else insisted upon, and Miss Moore neglected for
poets who ought not to be allowed to throw elegies in her grave.
I have read that several people think So-and-So the greatest
living woman poet; anybody would dislike applying so clumsy a

phrase to Miss Moore—but surely she is. Her poems, at their unlikely best, seem already immortal, objects that have endured their probative millenia in barrows; she has herself taken from them what time could take away, and left a skeleton the years can only harden. People have complained about the poems, in the words of the poems: "Why dissect destiny with instruments which are more specialized than the tissues of destiny itself?" But nothing is more specialized than destiny. Other people have objected, "They are so small." Yes, they are as small as those animals which save the foolish heroes of fairy tales—which can save only the heroes, because they are too small not to have been disregarded by everyone else.

Her Shield

M ISS MOORE'S poems judge what is said about them
almost as much as poems can, so that even one's praise
is hesitant, uncertain of its welcome. As her readers know, her
father used to say, "The deepest feeling always shows itself in
silence;/ not in silence, but restraint"; and she herself has said,
"If tributes cannot/ be implicit, give me diatribes and the fra-
grance of iodine." Quotation is a tribute as near implicit as I can
get; so I will quote where I can, and criticize where I can't. (My
father used to say, "The deepest feeling always shows itself in
scratches;/ not in scratches, but in iodine.") And I have found
one little hole through which to creep to criticism, Miss Moore's
"If he must give an opinion it is permissible that the/ critic
should know what he likes." I know; and to have to give an
opinion is to be human. Besides, I have never believed her father
about feeling; "entire affection hateth nicer hands," as Spenser
says, and I should hate to trust to "armour's undermining
modesty/ instead of innocent depravity." And that last quotation isn't Spenser.

It felt queer to see all over again this year, in English reviews of Miss Moore's *Collected Poems*, those sentences—sentences once so familiarly American—saying that she isn't a poet at all. I can understand how anyone looking into her book for the first time, and coming on an early passage like "Disbelief and conscious fastidiousness were the staple/ ingredients in its/ disinclination to move. Finally its hardihood was/ not proof against its/ proclivity to more fully appraise such bits/ of food as the stream/ bore counter to it," might make this mistake; but what goes on in the mind that experiences

> *And Bluebeard's Tower above the coral-reefs,*
> *the magic mouse-trap closing on all points of the compass,*
> *capping like petrified surf the furious azure of the bay,*
> *where there is no dust, and life is like a lemon-leaf,*
> *a green piece of tough translucent parchment,*

and, dissatisfied, decides that it is prose? Aren't these lines (ordinary enough lines for her) the work of someone even at first glance a poet, with the poet's immemorial power to make the things of this world seen and felt and living in words? And even if the rhythms were those of prose—these are not—wouldn't we rather have poetry in prose than prose in verse? I wouldn't trade *Prudence is a rich, ugly old maid courted by Incapacity* for some epics.

Nowadays, over here, Miss Moore wins all the awards there are; but it took several decades for what public there is to get used to her—she was, until very recently, read unreasonably little and praised reasonably much. Even the circumstances hindered. The dust-jacket of her *Collected Poems* says: "Since the former volumes are out of print many readers will now, for the first time, have the opportunity to own the treasure of her poetry." This *is* a felicitous way for a publishing firm to say that it has allowed to remain out of print, for many years, most of the poetry of one of the great living poets. Miss Moore's prose-seeming, matter-of-factly rhythmed syllabic verse, the odd look most of her poems have on the page (their unusual stanzaic patterns, their words divided at the ends of lines, give many of them a consciously, sometimes misleadingly experimental or modernist look), their almost ostentatious lack of transitions and explanations, the absence of romance and rhetoric, of acceptedly Poetic airs and properties, did most to keep conservative readers from liking her poetry. Her restraint, her lack—her wonderful lack—of arbitrary intensity or violence, of sweep and overwhelmingness and size, of cant, of sociological significance, and so on, made her unattractive both to some of the conservative readers of our age and to some of the advanced ones. Miss Moore was for a long time (in her own phrase about something else) "like Henry James 'damned by the public for decorum,'/ not decorum but restraint." She demands, "When I Buy Pictures," that the pictures "not wish to disarm anything." (Here I feel like begging for the pictures, in a wee voice: "Can't they be just a *little* disarming?" My tastes are less firmly classical.) The poems she made for herself were so careful never to wish to disarm anyone, to appeal to anyone's habitual responses and grosser instincts, to sweep anyone resistlessly away, that they seemed to most readers eccentrically but forbiddingly austere, so that the readers averted their faces from her calm, elegant, matter-of-fact face, so exactly moved and conscientiously unappealing as itself to seem averted. It was not the defects of her qualities but the qualities that made most of the public reluctant to accept her as more than a special case: her extraordinary discrimination, precision and restraint, the odd propriety of her imagination, her gifts of "natural promptness" (I use the phrase she found, but her own promptness is preternatural)—all these stood in her way and will go on standing in her way.

These people who *can't read modern poetry because it's so*— this or that or the other—why can't they read "Propriety" or "The Mind is an Enchanting Thing" or "What Are Years" or "The Steeple-Jack"? Aren't these plain-spoken, highly-formed, thoughtful, sincere, magnificently expressive—the worthy continuation of a great tradition of English poetry? Wouldn't the poet who wrote the *Horatian Ode* have been delighted with them? Why should a grown-up, moderately intelligent reader have any trouble with an early poem like, say, "New York"? The words that follow the title, the first words of the poem, are *the savage's romance*—here one stops and laughs shortly, as anybody but a good New Yorker will. (Her remark about Brooklyn, "this city of freckled/ integrity," has a more ambiguous face.) She goes on, by way of the fact that New York is the center of the wholesale fur trade, to the eighteenth century when furs were the link between the Five Nations and Bath, between Natty Bumppo and the Trianon:

> *It is a far cry from the "queen full of jewels"*
> *and the beau with the muff,*
> *from the gilt coach shaped like a perfume-bottle,*
> *to the conjunction of the Monongahela and the Allegheny,*

and the scholastic philosophy of the wilderness
to combat which one must stand outside and laugh
since to go in is to be lost.

And she finishes by saying about America—truthfully, one thinks and hopes—that "it is not the dime-novel exterior,/ Niagara Falls, the calico horses and the war-canoe" that matter, it is not the resources and the know-how, "it is not the plunder,/ but 'accessibility to experience.'"

The only way to combat a poem like this is to stand outside and laugh—to go in is to be lost, and in delight; how can you say better, more concretely and intelligently and imaginatively, what that long central sentence says? Isn't the word *scholastic* worth some books? Of course, if the eighteenth century and the frontier don't interest you, if you've never read or thought anything about them, the poem will seem to you uninteresting or incommunicative; but it is unreasonable to blame the poet for that. In grammar school, bent over the geography book, all of us lingered over the unexpected geometrical magnificence of "the conjunction of the Monongahela and the Allegheny," but none of the rest of us saw that it was part of a poem—our America was here around us, then, and we didn't know. And isn't the conclusion of Miss Moore's poem the best and truest case that can be made out for Americans?

It is most barbarously unjust to treat her (as some admiring critics do) as what she is only when she parodies herself: a sort of museum poet, an eccentric shut-in dealing in the collection, renovation, and exhibition of precise exotic properties. For she is a lot more American a writer (if to be an American is to be the heir, or heiress, of all the ages) than Thomas Wolfe or Erskine Caldwell or—but space fails me; she looks lovingly and knowingly at this "grassless/ linksless [no longer], languageless country in which letters are written/ not in Spanish, not in Greek, not in Latin, not in shorthand,/ but in plain American which cats and dogs can read!" Doesn't one's heart reverberate to that last phrase "as to a trumpet"?

Miss Moore is one of the most perceptive of writers, sees extraordinarily—the words fit her particularly well because of the ambiguity that makes them refer both to sensation and intelligence. One reads, at random among lines one likes: *But we prove, we do not explain our birth;* reads about the pangolin *returning before sunrise; stepping in the moonlight,/ on the moonlight peculiarly;* reads, *An aspect may deceive; as the/ elephant's columbine-tubed trunk/ held waveringly out—/ an at will heavy thing—is/ delicate./ Art is unfortunate./ One may be a blameless/ bachelor, and it is but a/ step to Congreve.* One relishes a fineness and strangeness and firmness of discrimination that one is not accustomed to, set forth with a lack of fuss that one is not accustomed to either; it is the exact opposite of all those novels which present, in the most verbose and elaborate of vocabularies, with the greatest and most obvious of pains, some complacently and irrelevantly Sensitive perceptions. How much has been left out, here! (One remembers Kipling's *A cut story is like a poked fire.*) What intelligence vibrates in the sounds, the rhythms, the pauses, in all the minute particulars that make up the body of the poem! The tone of Miss Moore's poems, often, is enough to give the reader great pleasure, since it is a tone of much wit and precision and intelligence, of irony and forbearance, of unusual moral penetration—is plainly the voice of a person of good taste and good sense and good will, of a genuinely human being. Because of the curious juxtaposition of curious particulars, most of the things that inhabit her poetry seem extraordinarily bright, exact, and there—just as unfamiliar colors, in unfamiliar combinations, seem impossibly vivid. She is *the* poet of the particular—or, when she fails, of the peculiar; and is also, in our time, *the* poet of general moral statement. Often, because of their exact seriousness of utterance, their complete individuality of embodiment, these generalizations of hers seem almost more particular than the particulars.

In some of her poems Miss Moore has discovered both a new sort of subject (a queer many-headed one) and a new sort of connection and structure for it, so that she has widened the scope of poetry; if poetry, like other organisms, wants to convert into itself everything there is, she has helped it to. She has shown us that the world is more poetic than we thought. She has a discriminating love of what others have seen and made and said, and has learned (like a burglar who marks everything that he has stolen with the owner's name, and then exhibits it in his stall in the marketplace) to make novel and beautiful use of such things in her own work, where they are sometimes set off by their surroundings, sometimes metamorphosed. But for Miss Moore I'd never have got to read about "the emerald's 'grass-lamp glow,' " or about the Abbé Berlèse, who said, "In the camellia-house there must be/ no smoke from the stove, or dew on/ the windows, lest the plants ail . . ./ mistakes are irreparable and nothing will avail," or about "our clasped

hands that swear, 'By Peace/ Plenty; as/ by Wisdom, Peace,' "
or about any of a thousand such things—so I feel as grateful to
her memory as to a novelist's. Novelists are the most remembering of animals, but Miss Moore comes next.

Her poems have the excellences not of some specialized,
primarily or exclusively Poetic expression, but of expression in
general; she says so many good things that, call it prose or
poetry or what you will, her work is wonderful. She says, for
instance:

> . . . *The polished wedge*
> *that might have split the firmament*
> *was dumb. At last it threw itself away*
> *and falling down, conferred on some poor fool, a privilege.*

Is this an aphorism in the form of a fable, or a fable in the form
of an aphorism? It doesn't matter. But how sadly and firmly
and mockingly *so* it is, whatever it is; we don't need to search
for an application.

Miss Moore speaks well, memorably well, unforgettably well,
in many different ways. She is, sometimes, as tersely conclusive
as Grimm:

> *Jacob when a-dying, asked*
> *Joseph: Who are these? and blessed*
> *both sons, the younger most, vexing Joseph. And*
> *Joseph was vexing to some* . . .

or as wise as Goethe:

> *Though white is*
> *the colour of worship and of mourning, he*

is not here to worship and he is too wise
to mourn,—a life prisoner but reconciled.
With trunk tucked up compactly—the elephant's
sign of defeat—he resisted, but is the child

of reason now. His straight trunk seems to say: when
what we hoped for came to nothing, we revived . . .

or as beguiling, as full of becoming propriety, as Beatrix Potter:

> *The fish-spine*
> *on firs, on*
> > *sombre trees*
> > *by the sea's*
> *walls of wave-worn rock—have it; and*
> *a moonbow and Bach's cheerful firmness*
> > *in a minor key.*
> > *It's an owl-and-a-pussy-*
>
> *both-content*
> *agreement.*
> > *Come, come. It's*
> > *mixed with wits;*
> *it's not a graceful sadness. It's*
> *resistance with bent head, like foxtail*
> > *millet's . . .*

or as purely magical as Alban Berg:

> *Plagued by the nightingale*
> *in the new leaves,*
> *with its silence—*

> *not its silence but its silences,*
> *he says of it:*
> *"It clothes me with a shirt of fire . . ."*

or as elevated as the Old Testament:

> *Sun and moon and day and night and man and beast*
>   *each with a splendour*
>   *which man in all his vileness cannot*
>   *set aside; each with an excellence! . . .*

or as morally and rhetorically magnificent as St. Paul, when she says about man, at the end of the best of all her poems, "The Pangolin":

>   *Un-*
>   *ignorant,*
>   *modest and unemotional, and all emotion,*
>   *he has everlasting vigour,*
>   *power to grow,*
>   *though there are few creatures who can make one*
>   *breathe faster and make one erecter.*

> *Not afraid of anything is he,*
>   *and then goes cowering forth, tread paced to meet an*
>   *obstacle*
> *at every step. Consistent with the*
>   *formula—warm blood, no gills, two pairs of hands and*
>   *a few hairs—that*
> *is a mammal; there he sits in his own habitat,*
>   *serge-clad, strong-shod. The prey of fear, he always*

curtailed, extinguished, thwarted by the dusk,
work partly done,
says to the alternating blaze,
"Again the sun!
anew each day; and new and new and new,
that comes into and steadies my soul."

The reader may feel, "You're certainly quoting a lot." But I
have only begun to quote—or wish that I had; these are just a
few of the things I can't bear not to quote, I haven't yet come
to the things I want to quote—I may never get to them. But how
can I resist telling you "that one must not borrow a long white
beard and tie it on/ and threaten with the scythe of time the
casually curious"? Or say nothing about the "swan, with swart
blind look askance/ and gondoliering legs" (the "swart blind
look askance" makes us not only see, but also feel ourselves
into, the swan); or about the jerboa that "stops its gleaning/
on little wheel castors, and makes fern-seed/ footprints with
kangaroo speed"; or about "this graft-grown briar-black
bloom"?—a phrase that would have made Hopkins say with a
complacent smile, "Now, *that's* the way you use words." But
there are hundreds of phrases as good or better: one goes
through "The Steeple-Jack" and "The Hero" hating to leave
anything unquoted. There "the/ whirlwind fife-and-drum of
the storm bends the salt/ marsh grass, disturbs stars in the sky
and the/ star in the steeple; it is a privilege to see so/ much
confusion"; there one finds "presidents who have repaid/ sin-
driven/ senators by not thinking about them"; there one hears

"the 'scare-babe voice'/ from the neglected yew set with/ the semi-precious cat's eyes of the owl"; there

> the decorous frock-coated Negro
>
> by the grotto
>
> answers the fearless sightseeing hobo
>> who asks the man she's with, what's this,
>> what's that, where's Martha
>> buried, "Gen-ral Washington
>> there; his lady, here"; speaking
>> as if in a play, not seeing her . . .

Even admiration seems superfluous. But expostulation doesn't: *where* is Ambrose the student, with his not-native hat? and the pitch, not true, of the church steeple? and that "elegance the source of which is not bravado" that we and the student like? I think that Miss Moore was right to cut "The Steeple-Jack"—the poem seems plainer and clearer in its shortened state—but she has cut too much: when the reader comes, at the end, to "the hero, the student, the steeple-jack, each in his way, is at home," he must go to the next poem for the hero, has lost the student entirely, and has to make out as best he can with the steeple-jack. I wish that the poet had cut only as far as "but here they've cats not cobras to keep out the rats"; this would keep the best things, the things necessary for the sense of the poem, and still get rid of the tropical digression. The reader may feel like saying, "Let her do as she pleases with the poem; it's hers, isn't it?" No; it's much too good a poem for that, it long ago became everybody's, and we can protest just as we could if Donatello cut off David's left leg.

. . .

The change in Miss Moore's work, between her earliest and latest poems, is an attractive and favorable change. How much more modernist, special-case, dryly elevated and abstract, she was to begin with! "As for butterflies, I can hardly conceive/ of one's attending upon you, but to question/ the congruence of the complement is vain, if it exists." Butter not only wouldn't melt in this mouth, it wouldn't go in; one runs away, an urchin in the gutter and glad to be, murmuring: "The Queen of Spain *has* no legs." Or Miss Moore begins a poem, with melting grace: "If yellow betokens infidelity,/ I am an infidel./ I could not bear a yellow rose ill will/ Because books said that yellow boded ill,/ White promised well." One's eyes widen; one sits the poet down in the porch swing, starts to go off to get her a glass of lemonade, and sees her metamorphosed before one's eyes into a new *Critique of Practical Reason*, feminine gender: for her next words are, "However, your particular possession,/ The sense of privacy,/ Indeed might deprecate/ Offended ears, and need not tolerate/ Effrontery." And that is all; the poem is over. Sometimes, in her early poems, she has not a tone but a manner, and a rather mannered manner at that—two or three such poems together seem a dry glittering expanse, i.e., a desert. But in her later work she often escapes entirely the vice most natural to her, this abstract, mannered, descriptive, consciously prosaic commentary (accompanied, usually, by a manneredness of leaving out all introductions and transitions and explanations, as if one could represent a stream by reproducing only the stepping-stones one crossed it on). As she says, compression is the first grace of style—is almost a defining characteristic of the poetry our age most admires; but such passages as those I am speaking of are not compressed—the time wasted on Being Abstract more than makes up for the time saved by leaving out. Looking at a poem like "What Are Years," we see how much her style has changed. And the changes in style represent a real change in the poet: when one is struck by the poet's seriousness and directness and lack of manner—by both her own individual excellence and by that anonymous excellence the best poets sometimes share—it is usually in one of the poems written during the '30's and '40's. I am emphasizing this difference too much, since even its existence is ignored, usually; but it is interesting what a different general impression the *Collected Poems* gives, compared to the old *Selected Poems*. (Not that it wasn't wonderful too.)

How often Miss Moore has written about Things (hers are aesthetic-moral, not commercial-utilitarian—they persist and reassure); or Plants (how can anything bad happen to a plant?); or Animals with holes, a heavy defensive armament, or a massive and herbivorous placidity superior to either the dangers or temptations of aggression. The way of the little jerboa on the sands—at once true, beautiful, and good—she understands; but the little shrew or weasel, that kills, if it can, two or three dozen animals in a night? the little larvae feeding on the still-living caterpillar their mother has paralyzed for them? Nature, in Miss Moore's poll of it, is overwhelmingly in favor of morality; but the results were implicit in the sampling—like the *Literary Digest*, she sent postcards to only the nicer animals. In these poems the lion never eats Androcles—or anything else except a paste of seeded rotten apples, the national diet of Erewhon; so that her truthful and surprising phrase, *the lion's ferocious chrysanthemum head*, may seem less surprising than it would for a wilder lion. Because so much of our own world is evil, she has transformed the Animal Kingdom, that amoral realm, into a realm of good; her consolatory, fabulous bestiary is more accurate than, but is almost as arranged as, any medieval one. We need it as much as she does, but how can we help feeling that she relies, some of the time, too surely upon this last version of pastoral? "You reassure me and people don't, except when they are like you—but really they are always like you," the poems say sometimes, to the beasts; and it is wonderful to have it said so, and for a moment to forget, behind the animals of a darkening landscape, their dark companions.

Some of the changes in Miss Moore's work can be considered in terms of Armour. Queer terms, you say? They are hers, not mine: a good deal of her poetry is specifically (and changingly) about armour, weapons, protection, places to hide; and she is not only conscious that this is so, but after a while writes poems about the fact that it is so. As she says, "armour seems extra," but it isn't; and when she writes about "another armoured animal," about another "thing made graceful by adversities, conversities," she does so with the sigh of someone who has come home. She asks whether a woman's looks are weapons or scalpels; comments, looking out on a quiet town: "It could scarcely be dangerous to be living/ in a town like this"; says about a man's nonchalance: "his by-/ play was more terrible in its effectiveness/ than the fiercest frontal attack./ The staff, the bag, the feigned inconsequence/ of manner, best bespeak that weapon, self-protectiveness." *That weapon, self-protectiveness!* The poet knows that morals are not "the memory of success that no longer succeeds," but a part of survival.

She writes: "As impassioned Handel/ . . . never was known to have fallen in love,/ the unconfiding frigate-bird hides/ in the height and in the majestic/ display of his art." If Handel (or the frigate-bird) had been less impassioned he wouldn't have hidden, and if his feelings had been less deep they'd have been expressed with less restraint, we are meant to feel; it was because he was so impassioned that he "never was known to have fallen in love," the poem almost says. And how much sisterly approval there is in that *unconfiding!* When a frigate-bird buys pictures, you can bet that the pictures "must not wish to disarm anything." (By being disarming we sometimes disarm others, but always disarm ourselves, lay ourselves open to rejection. But if we do not make ourselves disarming or appealing, everything can be a clear, creditable, take-it-or-leave-it affair, rejection is no longer rejection. Who would be such a fool as to make advances to his reader, advances which might end in rejection or, worse still, in acceptance?) Miss Moore spoke as she pleased, and did not care whether or not it pleased; mostly this made her firm and good and different, but sometimes it had its drawbacks.

She says of some armoured animals that they are "models of exactness." The association was natural: she thought of the animals as models and of the exactness as armour—and for such a writer, there was no armour like exactness, concision, irony. She wished to trust, as absolutely as she could, in flat laconic matter-of-factness, in the minimal statement, understatement: these earlier poems of hers approach as a limit a kind of ideal minimal statement, a truth thought of as underlying, prior to, all exaggeration and error; the poet has tried to strip or boil everything down to this point of hard, objective, absolute precision. But the most extreme precision leads inevitably to quotation; and quotation is armour and ambiguity and irony all at once—turtles are great quoters. Miss Moore leaves the stones she picks up carefully uncut, but places them in an unimaginably complicated and difficult setting, to sparkle under the Northern Lights of her continual irony. Nobody has ever been better at throwing away a line than this Miss Facing-Both-Ways, this La Rochefoucauld who has at last rid himself of La Rochefoucauld, and can disabusedly say about man:

> *he loves himself so much,*
> *he can permit himself*
> *no rival in that love . . .*

and about woman:

> *one is not rich but poor*
> *when one can always seem so right . . .*

and about both:

> *What can one do for them—*
> *these savages*
> *condemned to disaffect*
> *all those who are not visionaries*
> *alert to undertake the silly task*
> *of making people noble?*

All this is from "Marriage," the most ironic poem, surely, written by man or woman; and one reads it with additional pleasure because it was written by the woman who was later to say, so tenderly and magically: "What is more precise than precision? Illusion."

Along with precision she loved difficulty. She said about James and others: "It is the love of doing hard things/ that rebuffed and wore them out—a public out of sympathy with neatness./ Neatness of finish! Neatness of finish!" Miss Moore almost despairs of us in one poem, until she comes across some evidence which shows that, in spite of everything, "we are precisionists"; and Santa Claus's reindeer, in spite of cutwork ornaments and fur like eidelweiss, are still "rigorists," so she names the poem that for them. How much she cares for useless pains, difficulties undertaken for their own sake! Difficulty is the chief technical principle of her poetry, almost. (For sureness of execution, for originality of technical accomplishment, her poetry is unsurpassed in our time; Auden says almost that, and the author of "Under Sirius" ought to know. Some of her rhymes and rhythms and phrases look quite undiscoverable.) Such unnecessary pains, such fantastic difficulties! Yet with manners, arts, sports, hobbies, they are always there—so perhaps they are necessary after all.

But some of her earlier poems do seem "averted into perfection." You can't put the sea into a bottle unless you leave it open at the end, and sometimes hers is closed at both ends, closed into one of those crystal spheres inside which snowflakes are falling onto a tiny house, the house where the poet lives—or says that she lives. Sometimes Miss Moore writes about armour and wears it, the most delicately chased, live-seeming scale-armour anybody ever put together: armour hammered out of fern seed, woven from the silk of invisible cloaks—for it is almost, though not quite, as invisible as it pretends to be, and is

when most nearly invisible most nearly protecting. One is often
conscious while reading the poetry, the earlier poetry especially,
of a contained removed tone; of the cool precise untouchedness,
untouchableness, of fastidious rectitude; of innate merits and
their obligations, the obligations of ability and intelligence and
aristocracy—for if aristocracy has always worn armour, it has
also always lived dangerously: the association of aristocracy and
danger and obligation is as congenial to Miss Moore as is the
rest of the "flower and fruit of all that noted superiority." Some
of her poems have the manners or manner of ladies who learned
a little before birth not to mention money, who neither point nor
touch, and who scrupulously abstain from the mixed, live
vulgarity of life. "You sit still if, whenever you move, something jingles," Pound quotes an officer of the old school as saying. There is the same aristocratic abstention behind the restraint, the sitting still as long as it can, of this poetry. "The
passion for setting people right is in itself an afflictive disease./
Distaste which takes no credit to itself is best," she says in an
early poem; and says, broadly and fretfully for her, "We are
sick of the earth,/ sick of the pig-sty, wild geese and wild men."
At such moments she is a little disquieting (she speaks for everybody, in the best of the later poems, in a way in which she once
could not); one feels like quoting against her her own, "As if a
death-mask could replace/ Life's faulty excellence," and blurt-
ing that life-masks have their disadvantages too. We are uncomfortable—or else too comfortable—in a world in which feeling, affection, charity, are so entirely divorced from sexuality
and power, the bonds of the flesh. In this world of the poems
there are many thoughts, things, animals, sentiments, moral

203

insights; but money and passion and power, the brute fact that *works*, whether or not correctly, whether or not precisely—the whole Medusa-face of the world: these are gone. In the poem called "Marriage" marriage, with sex, children, and elementary economic existence missing, is an absurd unlikely affair, one that wouldn't fool a child; and, of course, children don't get married. But this reminds me how un-childish, un-young, Miss Moore's poems always are; she is like one of those earlier ages that dressed children as adults, and sent them off to college at the age of eleven—though the poems dress their children in animal-skins, and send them out into the wilderness to live happily ever after. Few poets have as much moral insight as Miss Moore; yet in her poems morality usually *is* simplified into self-abnegation, and Gauguin always seems to stay home with his family—which is right, but wrong in a way, too. Poems which celebrate morality choose more between good and evil, and less between lesser evils and greater goods, than life does, so that in them morality is simpler and more beautiful than it is in life, and we feel our attachment to it strengthened.

"Spine-swine (the edgehog misnamed hedgehog)," echidna, echinoderm, rhino, the spine pig or porcupine—"everything is battle-dressed"; so the late poem named "His Shield" begins. But by then Miss Moore has learned to put no trust in armour, says, "Pig-fur won't do, I'll wrap/ myself in salamander-skin like Presbyter John," the "inextinguishable salamander" who "revealed/ a formula safer than/ an armourer's: the power of relinquishing/ what one would keep," and whose "shield was his humility." And "What Are Years" begins "All are naked, none are safe," and speaks of overcoming our circumstances by accepting them; just as "Nevertheless" talks not about armour, not about weapons, but about what is behind or above them both: "The weak overcomes its/ menace, the strong over-/ comes itself. What is there/ like fortitude? What sap/ went through that little thread/ to make the cherry red!" All this is a wonderfully appealing, a disarming triumph; yet not so appealing, so disarming, so amused and imaginative and doubtful and tender, as her last look at armour, the last poem of her *Collected Poems*. It is called "Armour's Undermining Modesty"; I don't entirely understand it, but what I understand I love, and what I don't understand I love almost better. I will quote most of the last part of it:

> *No wonder we hate poetry,*
> *and stars and harps and the new moon. If tributes cannot*
> *be implicit,*
>
> > *give me diatribes and the fragrance of iodine,*
> > *the cork oak acorn grown in Spain;*
> > *the pale-ale-eyed impersonal look*
> > *which the sales-placard gives the bock beer buck.*
> *What is more precise than precision? Illusion.*
> *Knights we've known,*
>
> > *like those familiar*
> > *now unfamiliar knights who sought the Grail . . .*
>
> > *. . . did not let self bar*
> > *their usefulness to others who were*
> > *different. Though Mars is excessive*
> > *in being preventive,*

*heroes need not write an ordinall of attributes to enumerate
what they hate.*

> *I should, I confess,*
> *like to have a talk with one of them about excess,*
> *and armour's undermining modesty*
> *instead of innocent depravity.*
A mirror-of-steel uninsistence should countenance
continence,

> *objectified and not by chance,*
> *there in its frame of circumstance*
> *of innocence and altitude*
> *in an unhackneyed solitude.*
There is the tarnish; and there, the imperishable wish.

One doesn't need to say that this is one of Miss Moore's best
poems. Some of the others are, I think, "The Pangolin"; "Propriety" (if ever a poem was perfect "Propriety" is; how *could* a
poem end better?); "The Mind is an Enchanting Thing";
"Melancthon"; "Elephants"; the first half of "The Jerboa," that
poem called "Too Much"; "Spenser's Ireland"; "Bird-Witted";
"Smooth Gnarled Crape Myrtle"; "In Distrust of Merits";
"What Are Years"; "The Steeple-Jack"; "The Hero"; "Those
Various Scalpels"; "Marriage"; "His Shield"; and "New York."
"Virginia Britannia" is a beautiful poem that some of the time
gets lost in the maze of itself; "Nevertheless" and "No Swan So
Fine" are two of the most beautiful of the slighter poems;
"Camellia Sabina" is—but I must stop.

Miss Moore's *Collected Poems* is a neat little book, with all its

verse tucked into a hundred and thirty-eight pages; a reader
could, with a reference to size, rather easily put her into her
minor place, and say—as I heard a good or even great critic say
—that it is easy to see the difference between a poet like this and
a major poet. It is; is so easy that Miss Moore's real readers,
who share with her some of her "love of doing hard things,"
won't want to do it—not for a century or two, at least, and then
only with an indifferent, "I suppose so." There is so much of a
life concentrated into, objectified on, these hard, tender, serious
pages, there is such wit and truth and moral imagination in-
habiting this small space, that we are surprised at possibility,
and marvel all over again at the conditions of human making
and being. What Miss Moore's best poetry does, I can say best
in her words: it "comes into and steadies the soul," so that the
reader feels himself "a life prisoner, but reconciled."

From the Kingdom of Necessity

M ANY of the people who reviewed *Lord Weary's Castle* felt that it was as much of an event as Auden's first book; no one younger than Auden has written better poetry than the best of Robert Lowell's, it seems to me. Anyone who reads contemporary poetry will read it; perhaps people will understand the poetry more easily, and find it more congenial, if they see what the poems have developed out of, how they are related to each other, and why they say what they say.

Underneath all these poems "there is one story and one story only"; when this essential theme or subject is understood, the unity of attitudes and judgments underlying the variety of the poems becomes startlingly explicit. The poems understand the world as a sort of conflict of opposites. In this struggle one opposite is that cake of custom in which all of us lie embedded like lungfish—the statis or inertia of the stubborn self, the obstinate persistence in evil that is damnation. Into this realm of necessity the poems push everything that is closed, turned inward, incestuous, that blinds or binds: the Old Law, imperialism,

militarism, capitalism, Calvinism, Authority, the Father, the
"proper Bostonians," the rich who will "do everything for the
poor except get off their backs." But struggling within this like
leaven, falling to it like light, is everything that is free or open,
that grows or is willing to change: here is the generosity or open-
ness or willingness that is itself salvation; here is "accessibility to
experience"; this is the realm of freedom, of the Grace that has
replaced the Law, of the perfect liberator whom the poet calls
Christ.

Consequently the poems can have two possible movements or
organizations: they can move from what is closed to what is
open, or from what is open to what is closed. The second of these
organizations—which corresponds to an "unhappy ending"—is
less common, though there are many good examples of it: "The
Exile's Return," with its menacing *Voi ch'entrate* that transforms the exile's old home into a place where even hope must be
abandoned; the harsh and extraordinary "Between the Porch
and the Altar," with its four parts each ending in constriction
and frustration, and its hero who cannot get free of his mother,
her punishments, and her world even by dying, but who sees
both life and death in terms of her, and thinks at the end that,
sword in hand, the Lord "watches me for Mother, and will turn/
The bier and baby-carriage where I burn."

But normally the poems move into liberation. Even death is
seen as liberation, a widening into darkness: that old closed
system Grandfather Arthur Winslow, dying of cancer in his ad-
justed bed, at the last is the child Arthur whom the swanboats
once rode through the Public Garden, whom now "the ghost of
risen Jesus walks the waves to run/ Upon a trumpeting black

swan/ Beyond Charles River and the Acheron/ Where the wide waters and their voyager are one." (Compare the endings of "The Drunken Fisherman" and "Dea Roma.") "The Death of the Sheriff" moves from closure—the "ordered darkness" of the homicidal sheriff, the "loved sightless smother" of the incestuous lovers, the "unsearchable quicksilver heart/ Where spiders stare their eyes out at their own/ Spitting and knotted likeness" —up into the open sky, to those "light wanderers" the planets, to the "thirsty Dipper on the arc of night." Just so the cold, blundering, iron confusion of "Christmas Eve 'Under Hooker's Statue" ends in flowers, the wild fields, a Christ "once again turned wanderer and child." In "Rebellion" the son seals "an everlasting pact/ With Dives to *contract*/ The world that *spreads* in pain"; but at last he rebels against his father and his father's New England commercial theocracy, and "the world *spread*/ When the clubbed flintlock broke my father's brain." The italicized words ought to demonstrate how explicitly, at times, these poems formulate the world in the terms that I have used.

"Where the Rainbow Ends" describes in apocalyptic terms the wintry, Calvinist, capitalist—Mr. Lowell has Weber's unconvincing belief in the necessary connection between capitalism and Calvinism—dead end of God's covenant with man, a frozen Boston where even the cold-blooded serpents "whistle at the cold." (The poems often use cold as a plain and physically correct symbol for what is constricted or static.) There "the scythers, Time and Death,/ Helmed locusts, move upon the tree of breath," of the spirit of man; a bridge curves over Charles River like an ironic parody of the rainbow's covenant; both "the wild ingrafted olive and its root/ Are withered" [these are

Paul's terms for the Judaism of the Old Law and the Gentile Christianity grafted upon it]; "every dove [the Holy Ghost, the bringer of the olive leaf to the Ark] is sold" for a commercialized, legalized sacrifice. The whole system seems an abstract, rationalized "graph of Revelations," of the last accusation and judgment brought against man now that "the Chapel's sharp-shinned eagle shifts its hold/ On serpent-Time, the rainbow's epitaph." This last line means what the last line in "The Quaker Graveyard"—"The Lord survives the rainbow of His will"—means; both are inexpressibly menacing, since they show the covenant as something that binds only us, as something abrogated merely by the passage of time, as a closed system opening not into liberation but into infinite and overwhelming possibility; they have something of the terror, but none of the pity, of Blake's "Time is the mercy of Eternity."

Then the worshipper, like a victim, climbs to the altar of the terrible I AM, to breathe there the rarefied and intolerable ether of his union with the divinity of the Apocalypse; he despairs even of the wings that beat against his cheek: "What can the dove of Jesus give/ You now but wisdom, exile?" When the poem has reached this point of the most extreme closure, when the infinite grace that atones and liberates is seen as no more than the acid and useless wisdom of the exile, it opens with a rush of acceptant joy into: "Stand and live,/ The dove has brought an olive branch to eat." The dove of Jesus brings to the worshipper the olive branch that shows him that the flood has receded, opening the whole earth for him; it is the olive branch of peace and reconciliation, the olive branch that he is "to eat" as a symbol of the eaten flesh of Christ, of atonement, identification, and liberation. Both the old covenant and the new still hold, nothing has changed: here as they were and will be—says the poem—are life and salvation.

Mr. Lowell's Christianity has very little to do with the familiar literary Christianity of *as if*, the belief in the necessity of belief; and it is a kind of photographic negative of the faith of the usual Catholic convert, who distrusts freedom as much as he needs bondage, and who sees the world as a liberal chaos which can be ordered and redeemed only by that rigid and final Authority to Whom men submit without question. Lowell reminds one of those heretical enthusiasts, often disciplined and occasionally sanctified or excommunicated, who are more at home in the Church Triumphant than in the church of this world, which is one more state. A phrase like Mr. Lowell's "St. Peter, the distorted key" is likely to be appreciated outside the church and overlooked inside it, *ad maiorem gloriam* of Catholic poetry. All Mr. Lowell's earliest poems would seem to suggest that he was, congenitally, the ideal follower of Barth or Calvin: one imagines him, a few years ago, supporting neither Franco nor the loyalists, but yearning to send a couple of clippers full of converted minute-men to wipe out the whole bunch—human, hence deserving. (I wish that he could cast a colder eye on minute-men; his treatment of the American Revolution is in the great tradition of Marx, Engels, and Parson Weems.) Freedom is something that he has wished to escape into, by a very strange route. In his poems the Son is pure liberation from the incestuous, complacent, inveterate evil of established society, of which the Law is a part—although the Father, Jehovah, has retained both the violence necessary to break up this inertia and a good deal of the menacing sternness of Authority as such, just as the poems themselves have. It is interesting to compare the figure of the Uncle in early Auden, who sanctifies rebellion by his authority; the authority of Mr. Lowell's Christ is sanctified by his rebellion or liberation.

Anyone who compares Mr. Lowell's earlier and later poems will see this movement from constriction to liberation as his work's ruling principle of growth. The grim, violent, sordid constriction of his earliest poems—most of them omitted from *Lord Weary's Castle*—seems to be temperamental, the Old Adam which the poet grew from and only partially transcends; and a good deal of what is excessive in the extraordinary rhetorical machine of a poem like "The Quaker Graveyard at Nantucket," which first traps and then wrings to pieces the helpless reader— who rather enjoys it—is gone from some of his later poems, or else dramatically justified and no longer excessive. "The Quaker Graveyard" is a baroque work, like *Paradise Lost*, but all the *extase* of baroque has disappeared—the coiling violence of its rhetoric, the harsh and stubborn intensity that accompanies all its verbs and verbals, the clustering stresses learned from ac- centual verse, come from a man contracting every muscle, grinding his teeth together till his shut eyes ache. Some of Mr. Lowell's later work moved, for a while, in the direction of the poem's quiet contrast-section, "Walsingham"; the denunciatory prophetic tone disappeared, along with the savagely satiric effects that were one of the poet's weaknesses. Some of the later poems depend less on rhetorical description and more on dra- matic speech; their wholes have escaped from the hypnotic bondage of the details. Often the elaborate stanzas have changed into a novel sort of dramatic or narrative couplet, run-on but with heavily stressed rhymes. A girl's nightmare, in the late "Katherine's Dream," is clear, open, and speech-like, compared to the poet's own descriptive meditation in an earlier work like "Christmas at Black Rock."

Mr. Lowell has a completely unscientific but thoroughly historical mind. It is literary and traditional as well; he can use the past so effectively because he thinks so much as it did. He seems to be condemned both to read history and to repeat it. His present contains the past—especially Rome, the late Middle Ages, and a couple of centuries of New England—as an operative skeleton just under the skin. (This is rare among contemporary poets, who look at the past more as Blücher is supposed to have looked at London: "What a city to sack!") War, Trade, and Jehovah march side by side through all Mr. Lowell's ages: it is the fundamental likeness of the past and present, and not their disparity, which is insisted upon. "Cold/ Snaps the bronze toes and fingers of the Christ/ My father fetched from Florence, and the dead/ Chatters to nothing in the thankless ground/ His father screwed from Charlie Stark and sold/ To the selectmen." Here is a good deal of the history of New England's nineteenth century in a sentence.

Of New England Mr. Lowell has the ambivalent knowledge one has of one's damned kin. The poems are crowded with the "fearful Witnesses" who "fenced their gardens with the Red-man's bones"; the clippers and the slavers, their iron owners, and their old seamen knitting at the asylum; the Public Garden "where/ The bread-stuffed ducks are brooding, where with tub/ And strainer the mid-Sunday Irish scare/ The sun-struck shallows for the dusky chub"; the faith "that made the Pilgrim Makers take a lathe/ To point their wooden steeples lest the Word be dumb." Here his harshest propositions flower out of facts. But some of his earlier satires of present-day politics and its continuation have a severe crudity that suggest Michael Wigglesworth rewriting the "Horatian Ode"; airplanes he treats as Allen Tate does, only more so—he gives the impression of having encountered them in Mother Shipton. But these excesses were temporary; what is permanently excessive is a sort of obstinate violence or violent obstinacy of temperament and perception—in a day when poets long to be irresistible forces, he is an immovable object.

Mr. Lowell's period pieces are notable partly for their details—which are sometimes magically and professionally illusionary—and partly for the empathy, the historical identification, that underlie the details. These period pieces are intimately related to his adaptations of poems from other languages; both are valuable as ways of getting a varied, extensive, and alien experience into his work. Dismissing these adaptations as misguided "translations" is like dismissing "To Celia" or *Cathay*, and betrays an odd dislike or ignorance of an important and traditional procedure of poets.

Mr. Lowell is a thoroughly professional poet, and the degree of intensity of his poems is equalled by their degree of organization. Inside its elaborate stanzas the poem is put together like a mosaic: the shifts of movement, the varied pauses, the alternation in the length of sentences, and the counterpoint between lines and sentences are the outer form of a subject matter that has been given a dramatic, dialectical internal organization; and

it is hard to exaggerate the strength and life, the constant richness and surprise of metaphor and sound and motion, of the
language itself. The organization of the poems resembles that of
a great deal of traditional English poetry—especially when
compared to that type of semi-imagist modern organization in
which the things of a poem seem to marshal themselves like
Dryden's atoms—but often this is complicated by stream-of-
consciousness, dream, or dramatic-monologue types of structure.
This makes the poems more difficult, but it is worth the price—
many of the most valuable dramatic effects can hardly be at-
tained inside a more logical or abstract organization. Mr.
Lowell's poetry is a unique fusion of modernist and traditional
poetry, and there exist side by side in it certain effects that one
would have thought mutually exclusive; but it is essentially a
post- or anti-modernist poetry, and as such is certain to be influential.

This poet is wonderfully good at discovering powerful,
homely, grotesque, but exactly appropriate particulars for his
poems. "Actuality is something brute," said Peirce. "There is no
reason in it. I instance putting your shoulder against a door and
trying to force it open against an unseen, silent, and unknown
resistance." The things in Mr. Lowell's poems have, necessarily,
been wrenched into formal shape, organized under terrific
pressure, but they keep to an extraordinary degree their stubborn, unmoved toughness, their senseless originality and contingency: no poet is more notable for what, I have read, Duns
Scotus calls *haeccitas*—the contrary, persisting, and singular
thinginess of every being in the world; but this detailed factu-
ality is particularly effective because it sets off, or is set off by,

the elevation and rhetorical sweep characteristic of much earlier English poetry. Mr. Lowell is obviously a haptic rather than a visual type: a poem like "Colloquy in Black Rock" has some of the most successful kinaesthetic effects in English. It is impossible not to notice the weight and power of his lines, a strength that is sometimes mechanical or exaggerated, and sometimes overwhelming. But because of this strength the smooth, calm, and flowing ease of a few passages, the flat and colloquial ease of others, have even more effectiveness than they ordinarily would have: the dead mistress of Propertius, a black nail dangling from a finger, Lethe oozing from her nether lip, in the end can murmur to the "apple-sweetened Anio":

> . . . Anio, you will please
> Me if you whisper upon sliding knees:
> "Propertius, Cynthia is here:
> She shakes her blossoms when my waters clear."

Mr. Lowell, at his best and latest, is a dramatic poet: the poet's generalizations are usually implied, and the poem's explicit generalizations are there primarily because they are dramatically necessary—it is not simply the poet who means them. He does not present themes or generalizations but a world; the differences and similarities between it and ours bring home to us themes, generalizations, and the poet himself. It is partly because of this that atheists are vexed by his Catholic views (and Catholics by his heretical ones) considerably less than they normally would be.

But there are other reasons. The poet's rather odd and imaginative Catholicism is thoroughly suitable to his mind, which is so traditional, theocentric, and anthropomorphic that no images from the sciences, next to none from philosophy, occur in his poems. Such a Catholicism is thoroughly suited to literature, since it *is* essentially literary, anthropomorphic, emotional. It is an advantage to a poet to have a frame of reference, terms of generalization, which are themselves human, affective, and effective as literature. *Bodily Changes in Fear, Rage, Pain, and Hunger* may let the poet know more about the anger of Achilles, but it is hard for him to have to talk about adrenalin and the thalamus; and when the arrows of Apollo are transformed into a "lack of adequate sanitary facilities," everything is lost but understanding. (This helps to explain the dependence of contemporary poetry on particulars, emotions, things—its generalizations, where they are most effective, are fantastic, though often traditionally so.) Naturally the terms of scientific explanation cannot have these poetic and emotional effects, since it is precisely by the exclusion of such effects that science has developed. (Many of the conclusions of the sciences are as poetic as anything in the world, but they have been of little use to poets—how can you use something you are delighted never to have heard of?) Mr. Lowell's Catholicism represents effective realities of human behavior and desire, regardless of whether it is true, false, or absurd; and, as everyone must realize, it is possible to tell part of the truth about the world in terms that are false, limited, and fantastic—else how should we have told it? There is admittedly no "correct" or "scientific" view of a great many things that a poet writes about, and he has to deal with them in dramatic and particular terms, if he has foregone the advantage of pre-scientific ideologies like Christianity or Marxism. Of course it seems to me an advantage that he can well forego; I remember writing about contemporary religious poems, "It is hard to enjoy the ambergris for thinking of all those suffering whales," and most people will feel this when they encounter a passage in Mr. Lowell's poetry telling them how Bernadette's miraculous vision of Our Lady "puts out reason's eyes." It does indeed.

It is unusually difficult to say which are the best poems in *Lord Weary's Castle:* several are realized past changing, successes that vary only in scope and intensity—others are poems that almost any living poet would be pleased to have written. But certainly some of the best things in the book are "Colloquy in Black Rock," "Between the Porch and the Altar," the first of the two poems that compose "The Death of the Sheriff," and "Where the Rainbow Ends"; "The Quaker Graveyard at Nantucket" and "At the Indian-Killer's Grave" have extremely good parts; some other moving, powerful, and unusual poems are "Death from Cancer," "The Exile's Return," "Mr. Edwards and the Spider," and "Mary Winslow"—and I hate to leave entirely unmentioned poems like "After the Surprising Conversions," "The Blind Leading the Blind," "The Drunken Fisherman," and "New Year's Day."

When I reviewed Mr. Lowell's first book I finished by saying, "Some of the best poems of the next years ought to be written by him." The appearance of *Lord Weary's Castle* makes me feel less like Adams or Leverrier than like a rain-maker who predicts rain and gets a flood which drowns everyone in the county. One or two of these poems, I think, will be read as long as men remember English.

Poets

I N JOSEPHINE MILES'S poems some overspecialized sensitivity and ability come to a cautionary end: mostly because Miss Miles asks surprisingly little of herself, and seems to feel that the world and poetry ask even less. Each of the poems in *Local Measures*—an acute title—fits conveniently on a single page: the poem is not the worked-out, required, sometimes lengthy expression of a subject that is trying to realize itself through Miss Miles, but only one more product of the Miles method for turning out Miles poems. These seem easily different from anybody else's poems, but hardly distinguishable from one another; their language, tone, and mechanism of effect have a relishingly idiosyncratic and monotonous regularity, as if they were the diary some impressionable but unimpassioned monomaniac had year by year been engraving on the side of a knitting-needle. Miss Miles specializes in the sly, dry, minimal observation. The poems are full of the conversational elegance of understatement, of a carefully awkward and mannered charm. Everything is just a little off; is, always, the precisely unexpected: so that after a while it becomes the expected, and the repetitions of words, the omissions of words or phrases required by ordinary syntax, the little voluntary tricks of technique seem as automatic as the emotions or ideas they accompany. Certainly the poems are "sincere" (else why say no more than this?); sometimes the phrases are good and the perceptions real, and I suppose it is nicer to have them come to nothing by Miss Miles's private formula than by one bought from the authorities of the day. But she is sadly bureaucratized. To write really good poems, not her carefully individualized, cultivated, limited affairs, she would need to have a change of heart—or else spend years on a corrective, some violent emotional epic, and thus in the end be dragged back to a better and more ordinary sort of poetry. But in some way she must come to be possessed by her daemon, instead of possessing him so complacently.

Adam Drinan's *Women of the Happy Island* is unusual and attractive. It is half prose and half poetry: the poems are said by the people of a small Scotch island, and the prose—which is better than the poetry, generally—tells you who says the poem, and where, and how. The poems are extremely uneven in technique and realization; they have many faults, but they also have enough affection and knowledge to convince you that Mr. Drinan is a writer in the sense in which it matters to be one. If he could get into his poems everything that is in his prose he would be a good poet. As it is, it is a pleasure to read a new poet who understands and cares for people and the world, instead of language and rhetoric and allusions, the rules and writers of the fashionable schools. It would take a good deal of quotation to convey the freshness and honesty of some of this writing, its closeness to what it describes; when you finish Mr. Drinan's book you have read little good poetry, but you have seen the things of his book as they are, and known his island. A girl writes home from the war, and says that she

> . . . *never again will loiter down to the shore*
> *clapping my hands and whistling and calling*
> *to the men-faced seals on the skerries any more . . .*

> . . . *nor watch them heaving on their clumsy hands . . .*

> . . . *For I have looked, O mother in whose breast*
> *I used to hide my face when I was frightened,*
> *on men that had been burned alive,*
> *their hands bent and fingers fused like flippers,*
> *Their not quite human features not quite seals'.*

These last two lines are true poetry. And Mr. Drinan begins his book:

(Over this island the wind sweeps continuously . . . Sometimes it passes angrily and with noise; sometimes it crawls almost imperceptibly, sometimes it seems to disappear altogether. But always it is passing over.

At the moment the wind is soft and leisurely. The daylight is fading from the levels at which people live. Up a pass from one house-studded bay to another, two figures are walking, a man and a woman, like ants on a knucklebone.

In the western entrance to the pass the sun sets: in the eastern entrance the moon rises.)

Anyone at all interested in poetry should buy Robert Graves' *Poems 1938–45* (just as he should buy William Carlos Williams' *Paterson: Part I* and Elizabeth Bishop's *North and South*), if only to get one poem, "To Juan at the Winter Solstice." It is one of the most beautiful poems of our century. Naturally, such a piece is far and away the best poem in the book; but the other poems are a pleasure to read even when they are inconsequential—their texture is so accomplished and personal, so terse, self-sufficient, and dryly or grotesquely or individually necessary, that the reader has the superstitious and wholly mistaken impression that the mediocre ones are mediocre only because Mr. Graves hasn't bothered to write anything so vulgar, modern, and alienated-from-himself as a successful poem. The technique of the poems is unusually objective and "classical"—a great deal of English and classical poetry is responsible for the way in which they are written—since metres and forms are things Mr. Graves can accept and transform as easily as he accepts and transforms the ghosts and gods and other historical beings that live on in the enchanting Hades of his novels; but what the poems say is sometimes wonderfully and sometimes rather disastrously the expression of his own peculiar being. He says that he writes poetry only for poets—but sometimes he writes it for one poet, and it is only as we approximate to that poet that we get the full value of the poems. Still, his new poems generally are not so whimsical or special-case as most of his old ones: he hasn't withered into truth, but has been gnarled and warped and furrowed into an extraordinarily individual right-ness that is sometimes "true" as well. Most of what successful poems there are in this book are small-scale and one-sided, too close to the (often beautifully witty or odd) Satires and Gro-tesques which follow them; nevertheless, Mr. Graves is one of the few poets alive who can write a first-rate poem, and one of the very few who are getting better as they get older. If I were Clement Attlee I'd pension or imprison Mr. Graves to get him to write more poems: certainly either action would seem matter-of-course to Robert Graves.

Denis Devlin is plainly a writer of intelligence and informa-tion, and he has a gift for language—for MacNeice's language, especially; but it does not seem to me that he has yet managed to make a good poem out of what he has. He does not seem to have enough realization of the demands the poem makes upon the poet—the demands that exclude bad, mediocre, and a great many good details from the completed work. He concentrates from instant to instant upon the parts, usually very rhetorical parts, and lets the whole take care of itself; he has a distracting method, persisted in for its own sake, of continually thinking about other people's poems or remarks, his own historical or geographical or cultural information, and making so many overt or covert allusions to all this that the reader realizes he is being taken on an expensive, cultivated, expected series of digressions, a Grand Tour. There is something rhetorical, un-evenly assertive, and sophisticated about the poems; the poet is extraordinarily and preponderantly conscious of surfaces. It is unjust for the book's dust-jacket to tell readers that Mr. Devlin is a diplomat, since they have a fair chance of guessing that from the poems:

> . . . *Bolder than the peasant tiger whose autumn beauty*
> *Sags in the expletive kill, or the sacrifice*
> *Of death puffed positive in the stance of duty* . . .

Surely the English Triumvirate could have sued Mr. Devlin for all this—flattery. *Stance!* Why, this is Norpois' attitude to a cliché: one imagines Mr. Devlin shaking hands with the first Roosevelt and murmuring, "Bully!" At his best Mr. Devlin is very different; but he is always jarring in and out of fit— he has such an inveterate, insensate passion for bad rhetorical effects and other people's rhetorical effects that, after the hundredth mesmeric echo of MacNeice, it is hard not to forsake him for that better and far more sympathetic poet. One reads

> . . . *Come up! Up up! The thunder at one with your voices in*
> *order chants, things*
> *Are with you, rolling her rump, Earth in bacchantic rumbas*
> *grave swings* . . .

and reflects, "with an awed contempt," that Tennyson had to write "Locksley Hall," Auden his parody of it, and MacNeice his "Eclogue at Christmas," in order that this couplet and its wretched siblings might exist.

Mr. Devlin has, I think, a rather poor and arbitrary ear; but he needs to have an unusually good one, since he writes in everything from free verse to lines like those I have just quoted. In his poems there is too much conscious and jagged "brilliance," too much description for description's sake, too many adjectives;

calm or proportion or rightness is almost constitutionally lacking. Still, he is witty, knowing, and forceful; his worse poems, plainly, are his earlier ones; and few poets understand better just how complicated the world is. He is so extraordinarily uneven that it is not fair to judge him by the ludicrously quotable rhetoric which infests his book; it is fairest to think of his possibilities, which—one sees from the best fragments of his work—would be good if he could think less about himself and his audience and the way people write poetry, and more about his subject and its poem.

Paterson (*Book I*) seems to me the best thing William Carlos Williams has ever written; I read it seven or eight times, and ended lost in delight. It is a shame to write a little review of it, instead of going over it page by page, explaining and admiring. And one hates to quote much, since the beauty, delicacy, and intelligence of the best parts depend so much upon their organization in the whole; quoting from it is like humming a theme and expecting a hearer to guess from that its effect upon its third repetition in a movement. I have used this simile deliberately, because—over and above the organization of argument or exposition—the organization of *Paterson* is musical to an almost unprecedented degree: Dr. Williams introduces a theme that stands for an idea, repeats it over and over in varied forms, develops it side by side with two or three more themes that are being developed, recurs to it time and time again throughout the poem, and echoes it for ironic or grotesque effects in thoroughly incongruous contexts. Sometimes this is done with the greatest complication and delicacy; he wants to introduce a bird whose call will stand for the clear speech of nature, in the midst of all the confusion and ugliness in which men could not exist except for "imagined beauty where there is none": so he says in disgust, "Stale as a whale's breath: breath!/ Breath!" and ten lines later (during which three themes have been repeated and two of them joined at last in a "silent, uncommunicative," and satisfying resolution) he says that he has

> Only of late, late! begun to know, to
> know clearly (as through clear ice) whence
> I draw my breath or how to employ it
> clearly—if not well:
>
> Clearly!
> speaks the red-breast his behest. Clearly!
> clearly!

These double exclamations have so prepared for the bird's call that it strikes you, when you are reading the poem itself, like the blow which dissolves an enchantment. And really the preparation has been even more complicated: two pages before there was the line "divorce! divorce!" and, half a page before, the birds and weeds by the river were introduced with

> . . . white, in
> the shadows among the blue-flowered
> Pickerel-weed, in summer, summer! if it should
> ever come . . .

If you want to write a long poem which doesn't stick to one subject, but which unifies a dozen, you can learn a good deal from *Paterson*.

227

The subject of *Paterson* is: How can you tell the truth about things?—that is, how can you find a language so close to the world that the world can be represented and understood in it?

> *Paterson lies in the valley under the Passaic Falls*
> *its spent waters forming the outline of his back. He*
> *lies on his right side, head near the thunder*
> *of the water filling his dreams! Eternally asleep,*
> *his dreams walk about the city where he persists*
> *incognito. Butterflies settle on his stone ear.*

How can he—this city that is man—find the language for what he sees and is, the language without which true knowledge is impossible? He starts with the particulars ("Say it, no ideas but in things") which stream to him like the river, "rolling up out of chaos,/ a nine months' wonder"; with the interpenetration of everything with everything, "the drunk the sober; the illustrious/ the gross; one":

> *It is the ignorant sun*
> *rising in the slot of*
> *hollow suns risen, so that never in this*
> *world will a man live well in his body*
> *save dying—and not know himself*
> *dying . . .*

The water falls and then rises in "floating mists, to be rained down and/ regathered into a river that flows/ and encircles"; the water, in its time, is "combed into straight lines/ from that rafter of a rock's/ lip," and attains clarity; but the people are like flowers that the bee misses, they fail and die and "Life is sweet, they say"—but their speech has failed them, "they do not know the words/ or have not/ the courage to use them," and they hear only "a false language pouring—a/ language (misunderstood) pouring (misinterpreted) without/ dignity, without minister, crashing upon a stone ear." And the language available to them, the language of scholarship and science and the universities, is

> *a bud forever green*
> *tight-curled, upon the pavement, perfect*
> *in justice and substance but divorced, divorced*
> *from its fellows, fallen low—*
> > *Divorce is*
> *the sign of knowledge in our time,*
> *divorce! divorce!*

Girls walk by the river at Easter and one, bearing a willow twig in her hand as Artemis bore the moon's crescent bow,

> *holds it, the gathered spray,*
> *upright in the air, the pouring air,*
> *strokes the soft fur—*
> > *Ain't they beautiful!*

(How could words show better than these last three the touching half-success, half-failure of their language?) And Sam Patch, the professional daredevil who jumped over the Falls with his pet bear, could *say* only: "Some things can be done as well as others"; and Mrs. Cumming, the minister's wife, shrieked unheard and fell unseen from the brink; and the two were only

> *a body found next spring*
> *frozen in an ice-cake; or a body*
> *fished next day from the muddy swirl—*
>
> *both silent, uncommunicative.*

The speech of sexual understanding, of natural love, is represented by three beautifully developed themes: a photograph of the nine wives of a Negro chief; a tree standing on the brink of a waterfall; and two lovers talking by the river:

> *We sit and talk and the*
> *silence speaks of the giants*
> *who have died in the past and have*
> *returned to those scenes unsatisfied*
> *and who is not unsatisfied, the*
> *silent, Singac the rock-shoulder*
> *emerging from the rocks—and the giants*
> *live again in your silence and*
> *unacknowledged desire . . .*

But now the air by the river "brings in the rumors of separate worlds," and the poem is dragged from its highest point in the natural world, from the early, fresh, and green years of the city, into the slums of Paterson, into the collapse of this natural language, into a "delirium of solutions," into the back streets of that "great belly/ that no longer laughs but mourns/ with its expressionless black navel love's/ deceit." Here is the whole failure of Paterson's ideas and speech, and he is forced to begin all over; Part II of the poem ends with the ominous, "No ideas but/ in the facts."

Part III opens with this beautiful and unexpected passage:

> *How strange you are, you idiot!*
> *So you think because the rose*
> *is red that you shall have the mastery?*
> *The rose is green and will bloom,*
> *overtopping you, green, livid*
> *green when you shall no more speak, or*
> *taste, or even be. My whole life*
> *has hung too long upon a partial victory.*

The underlying green of the facts always cancels out the red in which we had found our partial, temporary, aesthetic victory; and the poem now introduces the livid green of the obstinate and contorted lives, the lifeless perversions of the industrial city. Here are the slums; here is the estate with its acre hothouse, weedlike orchids, and French maid whose only duty is to "groom/ the pet Pomeranians—who sleep"; here is the university with its clerks

> *spitted on fixed concepts like*
> *roasting hogs, sputtering, their drip sizzling*
> *in the fire*
>
> *Something else, something else the same.*

Then (in one of the fine prose quotations—much altered by the poet, surely—which interrupt the verse) people drain the lake there, all day and all night long kill the fish and eels with clubs, carry them away in baskets; there is nothing left but the mud. The sleeping Paterson, "moveless," envies the men who could run off "toward the peripheries—to other centers, direct," for some "loveliness and/ authority in the world," who could leap like Sam Patch and be found "the following spring, frozen in/ an ice cake." But he goes on thinking to a very bitter end, and reproduces the brutal ignorance of his city as something both horrible and pathetic:

> *And silk spins from the hot drums to a music*
> *of pathetic souvenirs, a comb and nail-file*
> *in an imitation leather case—to*
> *remind him, to remind him! and*
> *a photograph-holder with pictures of himself*
> *between the two children, all returned*
> *weeping, weeping—in the back room*
> *of the widow who married again, a vile tongue*
> *but laborious ways, driving a drunken*
> *husband . . .*

But he contrasts his own mystery, the mystery of people's actual lives, with the mystery that "the convent of the Little Sisters of/ St. Ann pretends"; and he understands the people "wiping the nose on sleeves, come here/ to dream"; he understands that

> *Things, things unmentionable*
> *the sink with the waste farina in it and*
> *lumps of rancid meat, milk-bottle-tops: have*
> *here a still tranquillity and loveliness . . .*

Then Paterson "shifts his change," and an earthquake and a "remarkable rumbling noise" frighten the city but leave it undamaged—this in the prose of an old newspaper account; and at the end of the poem he stands in the flickering green of the

cavern under the waterfall (the dark, skulled world of consciousness), hedged in by the pouring torrent whose thunder drowns
out any language: "The myth/ that holds up the rock,/ that
holds up the water thrives there—/ in that cavern, that profound cleft"; and the readers of the poem have shown to them,
in the last words of the poem,

> *standing, shrouded there, in that din,*
> *Earth, the chatterer, father of all*
> *speech. . . .*

It takes several readings to work out the poem's argument
(it is a poem that *must* be read over and over), and it seemed to
me that I could do most for its readers by roughly summarizing
that argument. There are hundreds of things in the poem that
deserve specific mention. The poem is weakest in the middle
of the third section—I'd give page numbers if New Directions
had remembered to put any in—but this seems understandable
and almost inevitable. Everything in the poem is interwoven
with everything else, just as the strands of the Falls interlace:
how wonderful and unlikely that this extraordinary mixture of
the most delicate lyricism of perception and feeling with the
hardest and homeliest actuality should ever have come into
being! There has never been a poem more American (though
the only influence one sees in it is that of the river scene from
Finnegans Wake); if the next three books are as good as this
one, which introduces "the elemental character of the place,"
the whole poem will be the best very long poem that any American has written.

. . .

233

The best poems in Elizabeth Bishop's *North and South* are so good that it takes a geological event like *Paterson* to overshadow them. "The Fish" and "Roosters" are two of the most calmly beautiful, deeply sympathetic poems of our time; "The Monument," "The Man-Moth," "The Weed," the first "Song for a Colored Singer," and one or two others are almost, or quite, as good; and there are charming poems on a smaller scale, or beautiful fragments—for instance, the end of "Love Lies Sleeping." Miss Bishop is capable of the most outlandish ingenuity—who else could have made a witty mirror-image poem out of the fact that we are bilaterally symmetrical?—but is grave, calm, and tender at the same time. It is odd how pleasant and sympathetic her poems are, in these days when many a poet had rather walk down children like Mr. Hyde than weep over them like Swinburne, and when many a poem is gruesome occupational therapy for a poet who stays legally innocuous by means of it. The poet whom the poems of *North and South* present or imply is as attractively and unassuming good as the poet of *Observations* and *What Are Years*—but simpler and milder, less driven into desperate straits or dens of innocence, and taking this Century of Polycarp more for granted. (When you read Miss Bishop's "Florida," a poem whose first sentence begins, "The state with the prettiest name," and whose last sentence begins, "The alligator, who has five distinct calls: friendliness, love, mating, war, and warning," you don't need to be told that the poetry of Marianne Moore was, in the beginning, an appropriately selected foundation for Miss Bishop's work.) Miss Bishop's poems are almost never forced; in her best work restraint, calm, and proportion are implicit in every detail of organization and workmanship.

Instead of crying, with justice, "This is a world in which no one can get along," Miss Bishop's poems show that it is barely but perfectly possible—has been, that is, for her. Her work is unusually personal and honest in its wit, perception, and sensitivity—and in its restrictions too; all her poems have written underneath, *I have seen it.* She is morally so attractive, in poems like "The Fish" or "Roosters," because she understands so well that the wickedness and confusion of the age can explain and extenuate other people's wickedness and confusion, but not, for you, your own; that morality, for the individual, is usually a small, personal, statistical, but heartbreaking or heart-warming affair of omissions and commissions the greatest of which will seem infinitesimal, ludicrously beneath notice, to those who govern, rationalize, and deplore; that it is sometimes difficult and unnatural, but sometimes easy and natural, to "do well"; that beneath our lives "there is inescapable hope, the pivot," so that in the revolution of things even the heartsick Peter can someday find "his dreadful rooster come to mean forgiveness"; that when you see the snapped lines trailing, "a five-haired beard of wisdom," from the great fish's aching jaw, it is then that victory fills "the little rented boat," that the oil on the bilgewater by the rusty engine is "rainbow, rainbow, rainbow!"—that you let the fish go.

Reading so much that is good, in this accidental three-months collection, has made me feel how strange it is that *our* age should have poets like these. Let me admit, very willingly, that some of our poets are the most difficult that any age has known; but why doesn't everybody admit what anybody must know?—that here and now most people can't and don't read poetry, that the shepherd or potboy of other ages liked and understood poetry better than the usual educated person does today. What does the public do for poets like Mr. Graves and Mr. Williams and Miss Bishop except grumble accusingly that it "can't understand them," neglecting to add that it can't understand Blake or Donne or Hopkins or Shakespeare either? Today poetry, like virtue, is its own reward; the poems of Miss Bishop or Mr. Williams or Mr. Graves are a lonely triumph of integrity, knowledge, and affection.

An Introduction to
the Selected Poems of
William Carlos Williams

AN INTRODUCTION to these poems can be useful to the reader in the way that an introduction to.Peirce or William James can be: the reader is entering a realm that has some of the confusion and richness of the world, and any sort of summary is useful that keeps him reassured for a while—after that the place is its own justification. But most readers will automatically make any adjustments they need to make for writers so outspoken, warm-hearted, and largely generous as Peirce and James and Williams. Their voices are introduction enough.

Anyone would apply to Williams—besides *outspoken, warmhearted,* and *generous*—such words as *fresh, sympathetic, enthusiastic, spontaneous, open, impulsive, emotional, observant, curious, rash, courageous, undignified, unaffected, humanitarian, experimental, empirical, liberal, secular, democratic.* Both what he keeps and what he rejects are unusual: how many of these words would fit the other good poets of the time? He was born younger than they, with more of the frontier about him, of the this-worldly optimism of the 18th century; one can imagine his reading *Rameau's Nephew* with delighted enthusiasm, but wading along in Karl Barth with a dour blank frown. (I don't mean altogether to dissociate myself from these responses.) And he is as Pelagian as an obstetrician should be: as he points to the poor red thing mewling behind plate-glass, he says with professional, observant disbelief: "You mean you think *that's* full of Original Sin?" He has the honesty that consists in writing down the way things seem to you yourself, not the way that they really must be, that they *are*, that everybody but a misguided idealist or shallow optimist or bourgeois sentimentalist *knows* they are. One has about him the amused, admiring, and affectionate certainty that one has about Whitman: *Why, he'd say anything*—creditable or discreditable, sayable or unsayable, so long as he believes it. There is a delightful generosity and extravagance about the man in and behind the poems: one is attracted to him so automatically that one is "reminded of a story" of how S—— was defined (quite unjustly) as the only man in the universe who didn't like William James.

A *Selected Poems* does far less than justice to Williams. Any fair selection would have to include his wonderful *Paterson* (*Part I*), which is itself a book; and Williams is one of those poets, like Hardy, whose bad or mediocre poems do repay reading and do add to your respect for the poet. Williams' bad poems are usually rather winning machine-parts minus their machine, irrepressible exclamations about the weather of the world, interesting but more or less autonomous and irrelevant entries in a Lifetime Diary. But this is attractive; the usual bad poem in somebody's *Collected Works* is a learned, mannered, valued habit, a habit a little more careful than, and a little emptier than, brushing one's teeth.

The first thing one notices about Williams' poetry is how radically sensational and perceptual it is: "Say it! No ideas but in things." Williams shares with Marianne Moore and Wallace Stevens a feeling that almost nothing is more important, more of a true delight, than the way things look. Reading their poems is one long shudder of recognition; their reproduction of things, in its empirical gaiety, its clear abstract refinement of presentation, has something peculiarly and paradoxically American about it— English readers usually talk about their work as if it had been produced by three triangles fresh from Flatland. All three of these poets might have used, as an epigraph for their poetry, that beautiful saying that it is nicer to think than to do, to feel than to think, but nicest of all merely to look. Williams' poems, so far as their spirit is concerned, remind one of Marianne Moore's "It is not the plunder,/ but 'accessibility to experience' "; so far as their letter is concerned, they carry scrawled all over them Stevens' "The greatest poverty is not to live/ In a physical world"—and Stevens continues, quite as if he were Williams looking with wondering love at all the unlikely beauties of the poor:

> *One might have thought of sight, but who could think*
> *Of what it sees, for all the ill it sees.*

All three poets did their first good work in an odd climate of poetic opinion. Its expectations of behavior were imagist (the poet was supposed to see everything, to feel a great deal, and to think and to do and to make hardly anything), its metrical demands were minimal, and its ideals of organization were mosaic. The subject of poetry had changed from the actions of men to the reactions of poets—*reactions* being defined in a way that left the poet almost without motor system or cerebral cortex. This easily led to a strange kind of abstraction: for what is more abstract than a fortuitous collocation of sensations? Stevens, with his passion for philosophy, order, and blank verse, was naturally least affected by the atmosphere of the time, in which he was at most a tourist; and Marianne Moore synthesized her own novel organization out of syllabic verse, extravagantly elaborated, half-visual patterns, and an extension of moral judgment, feeling, and generalization to the whole world of imagist perception. Williams found his own sort of imagism considerably harder to modify. He had a boyish delight and trust in Things: there is always on his lips the familiar, pragmatic, American *These are the facts*—for he is the most pragmatic of writers, and so American that the adjective itself seems inadequate . . . one exclaims in despair and delight: He is the America of poets. Few of his poems had that pure crystalline inconsequence that the imagist poem ideally has—the world and Williams himself kept breaking into them; and this was certainly their salvation.

Williams' poetry is more remarkable for its empathy, sympathy, its muscular and emotional identification with its subjects, than any modern poetry except Rilke's. When you have read *Paterson* you know for the rest of your life what it is like to be a waterfall; and what other poet has turned so many of his readers into trees? Occasionally one realizes that this latest tree of Williams' is considerably more active than anybody else's grizzly bear; but usually the identification is so natural, the feel or rhythm of the poem so hypnotic, that the problem of belief never arises. Williams' knowledge of plants and animals, our brothers and sisters in the world, is surprising for its range and intensity; and he sets them down in the midst of the real weather of the world, so that the reader is full of an innocent lyric pleasure just in being out in the open, in feeling the wind tickling his skin. The poems are full of "Nature": Williams has reproduced with exact and loving fidelity both the illumination of the letter and the movement of the spirit. In these poems emotions, ideals, whole attitudes are implicit in a tone of voice, in the feel of his own overheard speech; or are expressed in terms of plants, animals, the landscape, the weather. You see from his instructions "To a Solitary Disciple" that it is what the landscape does—its analogical, anthropomorphized life—that matters to Williams; and it is only as the colors and surfaces reveal this that they are important.

At first people were introduced into the poems mainly as overheard or overlooked landscape; they spread. Williams has the knowledge of people one expects, and often does not get, from doctors; a knowledge one does not expect, and almost never gets, from contemporary poets. (For instance, what is probably the best poem by a living poet, *Four Quartets*, has only one real character, the poet, and a recurrent state of that character which we are assured is God; even the ghostly mentor encountered after the air-raid is half Eliot himself, a sort of Dostoievsky double.) One believes in and remembers the people in Williams' poems, though they usually remain behavioristic, sharply observed, sympathetic and empathetic sketches, and one cannot get from these sketches the knowledge of a character that one gets from some of Frost's early dramatic monologues and narratives, from a number of Hardy's poems, or from Williams' detailed and conclusive treatment of the most interesting character in the poems, himself. Some of the narrative and dramatic elements of his poetry seem to have drained off into his fiction. Williams' attitude toward his people is particularly admirable: he has neither that condescending, impatient, Pharisaical dismissal of the illiterate mass of mankind, nor that manufactured, mooing awe for an equally manufactured Little or Common Man, that disfigures so much contemporary writing. Williams loves, blames, and yells despairingly at the Little Men just as naturally and legitimately as Saint-Loup got angry at the servants: because he *feels*, not just says, that the differences between men are less important than their similarities—that he and you and I, together, are the Little Men.

Williams has a real and unusual dislike of, distrust in, Authority; and the Father-surrogate of the average work of art has been banished from his Eden. His ability to rest (or at least to thrash happily about) in contradictions, doubts, and general guesswork, without ever climbing aboard any of the monumental certainties that go perpetually by, perpetually on time—this ability may seem the opposite of Whitman's gift for boarding every certainty and riding off into every infinite, but the spirit behind them is the same. Williams' range (it is roughly Paterson, that microcosm which he has half-discovered, half-invented) is narrower than Whitman's, and yet there too one is reminded of Whitman:

Williams has much of the freeness of an earlier America, though it is a freedom haunted about by desperation and sorrow. The little motto one could invent for him—*In the suburbs, there one feels free*—is particularly ambiguous when one considers that those suburbs of his are overshadowed by, are a part of, the terrible industrial landscape of northeastern New Jersey. But the ambiguity is one that Williams himself not only understands but insists upon: if his poems are full of what is clear, delicate, and beautiful, they are also full of what is coarse, ugly, and horrible. There is no optimistic blindness in Williams, though there is a fresh gaiety, a stubborn or invincible joyousness. But when one thinks of the poems, of Williams himself, in the midst of these factories, dumps, subdivisions, express highways, patients, children, weeds, and wild-flowers of theirs—with the city of New York rising before them on the horizon, a pillar of smoke by day, a pillar of fire by night; when one thinks of this, one sees in an ironic light, the flat matter-of-fact light of the American landscape, James' remark that America "has no ruins." America is full of ruins, the ruins of hopes.

There are continually apparent in Williams that delicacy and subtlety which are sometimes so extraordinarily present, and sometimes so extraordinarily absent, in Whitman; and the hair-raising originality of some of Whitman's language is another bond between the two—no other poet of Whitman's time could have written

The orchestra whirls me wider than Uranus flies,
It wrenches such ardors from me I did not know I possessed
*   them,*

243

*It sails me, I dab with bare feet, they are lick'd by the indolent
    waves,*
I am cut by bitter and angry hail, I lose my breath,
*Sleep'd amid honey'd morphine, my windpipe throttled in
    fakes of death,*
At length let up again to feel the puzzle of puzzles . . .

I suppose that the third line and the *fakes of death* are the most
extraordinary things in the passage; yet the whole seems more
overwhelming than they. In spite of their faults—some of them
obvious to, and some of them seductive to, the most foolish
reader—poets like Whitman and Williams have about them
something more valuable than any faultlessness: a wonderful
largeness, a quantitative and qualitative generosity.

Williams' imagist-objectivist background and bias have
helped his poems by their emphasis on truthfulness, exactness,
concrete "presentation"; but they have harmed the poems by
their underemphasis on organization, logic, narrative, generalization—and the poems are so short, often, that there isn't time
for much. Some of the poems seem to say, "Truth is enough"—
truth meaning *data brought back alive*. But truth isn't enough.
Our crudest demand for excitement, for the "actions of men," for
the "real story" of something "important," something strange—
this demand is legitimate because it is the nature of the animal,
man, to make it; and the demand can hardly be neglected so
much as a great deal of the poetry of our time—of the good
poetry of our time—has neglected it. The materials of Williams'
unsuccessful poems have as much reality as the brick one stum-
bles over on the sidewalk; but how little has been done to them!

—the poem is pieces or, worse still, a piece. But sometimes just enough, exactly as little as is necessary, has been done; and in these poems the Nature of the edge of the American city—the weeds, clouds, and children of vacant lots—and its reflection in the minds of its inhabitants, exist for good.

One accepts as a perfect criticism of his own insufficiently organized (*i.e.*, insufficiently living) poems Williams' own lines: "And we thought to escape rime/ by imitation of the senseless/ unarrangement of wild things—the stupidest rime of all"; and one realizes at the same time, with a sense of reassurance, that few people know better than Williams how sensible the arrangement of wild things often is. Williams' good poems are in perfect agreement with his own explanation of what a poem is:

A poem is a small (or large) machine made of words. When I say there's nothing sentimental about a poem I mean that there can be no part, as in any other machine, that is redundant . . . Its movement is intrinsic, undulant, a physical more than a literary character. Therefore each speech having its own character, the poetry it engenders will be peculiar to that speech also in its own intrinsic form. The effect is beauty, what in a single object resolves our complex feelings of propriety . . . When a man makes a poem, makes it, mind you, he takes words as he finds them interrelated about him and composes them—without distortion which would mar their exact significances—into an intense expression of his perceptions and ardors that they may constitute a revelation in the speech that he uses. It isn't what he *says* that counts as a work of art, it's what he makes, with such intensity of perception that it lives with an intrinsic movement of its own to verify its authenticity.

It is the opposition between the *without distortion* and the repeated *makes* of this passage that gives Williams' poetry the type of organization that it has.

One is rather embarrassed at the necessity of calling Williams original; it is like saying that a Cheshire Cat smiles. Originality is one of his major virtues and minor vices. One thinks about some of his best poems, *I've never read or imagined anything like this;* and one thinks about some of his worst, *I wish to God this were a little more like ordinary poetry.* He is even less logical than the average good poet—he is an intellectual in neither the good nor the bad sense of the word—but loves abstractions for their own sake, and makes accomplished, characteristic, inveterate use of them, exactly as if they were sensations or emotions; there is no "dissociation of sensibility" in Williams. Both generalizations and particulars are handled with freshness and humor and imagination, with a delicacy and fantasy that are especially charming in so vigorous, realistic, and colloquial a writer.

The mosaic organization characteristic of imagism or "objectivism" develops naturally into the musical, thematic organization of poems like *Paterson* (*Part I*); many of its structural devices are interestingly, if quite independently, close to those of *Four Quartets* and "Coriolan," though Eliot at the same time utilizes a good many of the traditional devices that Williams dislikes. A large-scale organization which is neither logical, dramatic, nor narrative is something that contemporary poetry has particularly desired; such an organization seems possible but improbable, does not exist at present, and is most nearly approached in *Four Quartets* and *Paterson* (*Part I*).

Williams' poems are full of imperatives, exclamations, trochees—the rhythms and dynamics of their speech are being insisted upon as they could not be in any prose. It is this insistence upon dynamics that is fundamental in Williams' reading of his own poems: the listener realizes with astonished joy that he is hearing a method of reading poetry that is both excellent —for these particular poems—and completely unlike anything he has ever heard before. About Williams' meters one remark might be enough, here: that no one has written more accomplished and successful free verse. It seems to me that ordinary accentual-syllabic verse, in general, has tremendous advantages over "free," accentual, or syllabic verse—in English, of course. But that these other kinds of verse, in some particular situations or with some particular materials, can work out better for some poets, is so plain that any assertion to the contrary seems obstinate dogmatism. We want to explain *why* Williams' free verse or Marianne Moore's syllabic verse is successful, not to make fools of ourselves by arguing that it isn't. The verse-form of one of their poems, as anyone can see, is essential to its success; and it is impossible to produce the same effect by treating their material in accentual-syllabic verse. Anyone can invent the genius who might have done the same thing even better in ordinary English verse, but he is the most fruitless of inventions.

Contemporary criticism has not done very well by Williams; most of the good critics of poetry have not written about him, and one or two of the best, when they did write, just twitched as if flies were crawling over them. Yvor Winters has been Williams' most valuable advocate, and has written extremely well about one side of Williams' poetry; but his praise has never had enough effect on the average reader, who felt that Williams came as part of the big economy-sized package that included Elizabeth Daryush, Jones Very, and Winters' six best students. The most important thing that criticism can do for a poet, while he is alive, is to establish that atmosphere of interested respect which gets his poems a reasonably careful reading; it is only in the last couple of years that any such atmosphere has been established for Williams.

Williams' most impressive single piece is certainly *Paterson* (*Part I*): a reader has to be determinedly insensitive to modern poetry not to see that it has an extraordinary range and reality, a clear rightness that sometimes approaches perfection. I imagine that almost any list of Williams' best poems would include the extremely moving, completely realized "The Widow's Lament in Springtime"; that terrible poem (XVIII in "Spring and All") that begins, *The pure products of America/ go crazy;* "The Yachts," a poem that is a paradigm of all the unjust beauty, the necessary and unnecessary injustice of the world; "These," a poem that is pure deprivation; "Burning the Christmas Greens"; the long poem (called "Paterson: Episode 17" in Williams' *Collected Poems*) that uses for a refrain the phrase *Beautiful Thing;* the unimaginably delicate "To Waken an Old Lady"; the poem that begins, *By the road to the contagious hospital;* the beautiful "A Unison," in which Nature is once again both ritual and myth; and, perhaps, "The Sea-Elephant," "The Semblables," and "The Injury." And how many other poems there are that one never comes on without pleasure!

That Williams' poems are honest, exact, and original, that some of them are really *good* poems, seems to me obvious. But in concluding I had rather mention something even more obvious: their generosity and sympathy, their moral and human attractiveness.

Three Books

RICHARD WILBUR is a delicate, charming, and skillful poet. His poéms not only make you use, but make you eager to use, words like *attractive* and *appealing* and *engaging*. His poems are often gay and often elegiac—almost professionally elegiac, sometimes; funny or witty; individual; beautiful or, at worst, pretty; accomplished in their rhymes and rhythms and language. Somebody said about Christopher Fry—and almost anybody must have felt it—"I don't think real poetry is ever as *poetic* as this." One feels this way about some of Mr. Wilbur's language (and about some of what he says, too; what poets say is often just part of their language); but generally his language has a slight incongruity or "offness," a skillful use of verbs and kinesthetic words, a relishable relishing texture, a sugar-coated-slap-in-the-face rhetoric, that produce a real though rather mild pleasure. The reader notices that the poet never gets so lost either in his subject or in his emotions that he forgets to mix in his usual judicious proportion of all these things; his manners and manner never fail.

Mr. Wilbur seems to be a naturally lyric or descriptive poet. His book is rather like a picture gallery—he often mentions painters—and his people are usually not much more than portions of landscapes or still-lifes. The poems are all Scenes, none of them dramatic; and if the reader feels that you can't look at the best sunset for more than a few minutes (but that people sometimes last for centuries), he is sure to start longing for a murder or a character—after thirty or forty pages of *Ceremony* he would pay dollars for one dramatic monologue, some blessed graceless human voice that has not yet learned to express itself so composedly as poets do.

When you read "The Death of a Toad," a poem that begins *A toad the power mower caught,/ Chewed and clipped of a leg, with a hobbling hop has got/ To the garden verge*, you stop to shudder at the raw being of the world, at all that *a hobbling hop* has brought to life—*that* toad is real, all right. But when you read on, when Mr. Wilbur says that the toad *dies/ Toward some deep monotone,/ Toward misted and ebullient seas/ And cooling shores, toward lost Amphibia's emperies*, you think with a surge of irritation and dismay, "So it was all only an excuse for some Poetry." Yet the same poet can say to a sycamore,

> *Sycamore, trawled by the tilt sun,*
> *Still scrawl your trunk with tattered lights, and keep*
> *The spotted toad upon your patchy bark,*
> *Baffle the sight to sleep,*
> *Be' such a deep*
> *Rapids of lacing light and dark . . .*

and can say about olive trees in the "heavy jammed excess" of southern France,

> *Even when seen from near, the olive shows*
> *A hue of far away. Perhaps for this*
> *The dove brought olive back, a tree that grows*
> *Unearthly pale, which ever dims and dries,*
> *And whose great thirst, exceeding all excess,*
> *Teaches the South it is not paradise.*

These quotations seem to me to have an easy and graceful beauty; and one is delighted with the wit and delicacy of a passage like

> . . . *Tom Swift has vanished too,*

> *Who worked at none but wit's expense*
> *Putting dirigibles together*
> *Out in the yard, in the quiet weather,*
> *Whistling beyond Tom Sawyer's fence.*

When someone apostrophizes an eggplant: "Natural pomp! Excessive Nightshade's Prince! Polished potato," or says about a bird's nest fallen from a tree, "Oh risk hallowed eggs, oh/ Triumph of lightness! Legerity begs no/ Quarter: my Aunt Virginia, when"—when anybody speaks so, you say to him: "Good old Marianne Moore! Isn't she wonderful?" But Mr. Wilbur is not influenced by her any more; I wish he were. His second book seems more affected by general Victorian poetic practice than by any live poet; the reader sometimes thinks in surprise, "Why would anybody want to write like that?" An ambitious and felt and thoughtful poem like his first book's "Water-Walker" (an animal-morality poem about St. Paul; it, like Elizabeth Bishop's beautiful animal-morality poem about St. Peter, is a member of a genre that Miss Moore discovered and perfected) is a partial failure, but surely anybody would rather have written it than some of Mr. Wilbur's slight and conventional successes.

Most of his poetry consents too easily to its own unnecessary limitations. An unusually reflective halfback told me that as a run develops there is sometimes a moment when you can "settle for six or eight yards, or else take a chance and get stopped cold or, if you're lucky, go the whole way." Mr. Wilbur almost always settles for six or eight yards; and so many reviewers have praised him for this that in his second book he takes fewer risks than in his first. (He is like one of those Southern girls to whom everybody north of Baltimore has said, "Whatever you do, *don't* lose that lovely Southern accent of yours"; after a few years they sound like Amos and Andy.) If I were those reviewers I would quote to Mr. Wilbur something queer and true that Blake said on the same subject: "You never know what is enough unless you know what is more than enough." Mr. Wilbur never goes too far, but he never goes far enough. In the most serious sense of the word he is not a very satisfactory poet. And yet he seems the best of the quite young poets writing in this country, poets considerably younger than Lowell and Bishop and Shapiro and Roethke and Schwartz; I want to finish by admiring his best poems, not by complaining about their limitations. But I can't blame his readers if they say to him in encouraging impatient voices: "Come on, *take a chance!*" If you never look *just* wrong to

your contemporaries you will never look just right to posterity—
every writer has to be, to some extent, sometimes, a law unto
himself.

Since Robert Lowell's *The Mills of the Kavanaughs* consists of
only seven poems—one tremendously long, four quite sizeable—
I can treat them one by one. "The Fat Man in the Mirror"
makes a better impression on you if you haven't read the strange
and beautiful Werfel poem on which it is based; this "imitation
after Werfel"—never was anything less imitative!—is a baroque,
febrile, Horowitz-Variations-on-*The-Stars-and-Stripes-Forever*
affair. Part I of "Her Dead Brother" is a restrained, sinister, and
extremely effective poem; the suicide-by-gas-stove Part II is
effective in some portions, but is mannered and violent—Part I
seems better off as the separate poem that it originally was. It
would be hard to write, read, or imagine a more nightmarish
poem than "Thanksgiving's Over." On one level it is a complete
success, and it is almost with a sigh of relief that one concludes
that it does not quite succeed on another level, that all this is
the possible with which art does not have to deal, not the prob-
able with which it must. Still, it is a frightening and impressive
—and in parts very moving—poem which anybody will want to
read. The organization and whole conception of "David and
Bathsheba in the Public Garden" are so mannered and idiosyncratic, so peculiar to Mr. Lowell, that the poem is spoiled, in
spite of parts as beautiful as that about the harvest moon.
Someone is sure to say about this poem that you can't tell David
from Bathsheba without a program: they both (like the majority
of Mr. Lowell's characters) talk just like Mr. Lowell.

I cannot think of any objection at all to "Mother Marie Therese" and "Falling Asleep over the Aeneid," and if I could I would be too overawed to make it. "Mother Marie Therese" is the best poem Mr. Lowell has ever written, and "Falling Asleep over the Aeneid" is—is better; *very* few living poets have written poems that surpass these. "Mother Marie Therese" is the most human and tender, the least specialized, of all Mr. Lowell's poems; it is warped neither by Doctrine nor by that doctrine which each of us becomes for himself; in it, for once, Mr. Lowell really gets out of himself. Sometimes the New Brunswick nun who is talking does sound like a not-too-distant connection of the Lowells, but generally she seems as much herself as porpoise-bellied Father Turbot, "his bald spot tapestried by colored glass," seems himself when he squeaks: "N-n-nothing is so d-dead/ As a dead S-s-sister." Certainly Father Turbot is real; the drowned Mother Superior ("reading Rabelais from her chaise,/ Or parroting the *Action Française*"; she who "half-renounced by Candle, Book, and Bell,/ Her flowers and fowling-pieces for the church"; she who saw that our world is passing, but "whose trust/ Was in its princes") is real; and the sixty-year-old nun who speaks the poem in grief for her is most real of all. One can judge something of her reality and of the quality of the poem simply by looking at the long passage with which the poem ends:

> *The bell-buoy, whom she called the Cardinal,*
> *Dances upon her. If she hears at all,*
> *She only hears it tolling to this shore,*
> *Where our frost-bitten sisters know the roar*

Of water, inching, always on the move
For virgins, when they wish the times were love,
And their hysterical hosannahs rouse
The loveless harems of the buck ruffed grouse
Who drums, untroubled now, beside the sea—
As if he found our stern virginity
Contra naturam. *We are ruinous;*
God's Providence through time has mastered us:
Now all the bells are tongueless, now we freeze,
A later advent, pruner of warped trees,
Whistles about our nunnery slabs, and yells,
And water oozes from us into wells;
A new year swells and stirs. Our narrow Bay
Freezes itself and us. We cannot say
Christ even sees us, when the ice floes toss
His statue, made by Hurons, on the cross
That Father Turbot sank on Mother's mound—
A whirligig! Mother, we must give ground,
Little by little; but it does no good.
Tonight, while I am piling on more driftwood,
And stooping with the poker, you are here,
Telling your beads; and breathing in my ear,
You watch your orphan swording at her fears.
I feel you twitch my shoulder. No one hears
Us mock the sisters, as we used to, years
And years behind us, when we heard the spheres
Whirring venite; *and we held our ears.*
My mother's hollow sockets fill with tears.

"Falling Asleep over the Aeneid" is as good—and as thoroughly and surprisingly organized—a poem about power and the self as any I can recall. Its subject matter and peculiar circumstances justify the harshness and violence, the barbarous immediacy, that often seem arbitrary in Mr. Lowell's poems; and these are set off by passages as tender and beautiful as this description of the dead Pallas:

> Face of snow,
> You are the flower that country girls have caught,
> A wild bee-pillaged honey-suckle brought
> To the returning bridegroom—the design
> Has not yet left it, and the petals shine;
> The earth, its mother, has, at last, no help:
> It is itself.

I have rarely had more of a sense of the terrible continuity of the world (and of the ego that learns neither from itself nor from the world what the dead face is made to tell Aeneas: "Brother, try,/ O child of Aphrodite, try to die:/ To die is life") than when I read the conclusion into which all the terms of the poem coalesce:

> Church is over, and its bell
> Frightens the yellowhammers, as I wake
> And watch the whitecaps wrinkle up the lake.
> Mother's great-aunt, who died when I was eight,
> Stands by our parlor sabre. "Boy, it's late.
> Vergil must keep the Sabbath." Eighty years!
> It all comes back. My Uncle Charles appears,
> Blue-capped and bird-like. Phillips Brooks and Grant

Are frowning at his coffin, and my aunt,
Hearing his colored volunteers parade
Through Concord, laughs, and tells her English maid
To clip his yellow nostril hairs, and fold
His colors on him. . . . It is I, I hold
His sword to keep from falling, for the dust
On the stuffed birds is breathless, for the bust
Of young Augustus weighs on Vergil's shelf:
It scowls into my glasses at itself.

I am not sure how good this passage will seem in isolation; as the ending of this poem, an ending with every term prepared for, every symbol established, it is as magnificent as it is final.

"The Mills of the Kavanaughs," the long narrative poem that fills half the book, is an interesting and powerful poem; but in spite of having wonderful lines and sections—many of both—it does not seem to me successful as a unified work of art, a narrative poem that makes the same sort of sense a novel or story makes. It is too much a succession of nightmares and daydreams that are half-nightmare; one counts with amusement and disbelief the number of times the poem becomes a nightmare-vision or its equivalent. And these are only too successfully nightmarish, so that there is a sort of monotonous violence and extremity about the poem, as if it were a piece of music that consisted of nothing but climaxes. The people too often seem to be acting *in the manner of* Robert Lowell, rather than plausibly as real people act (or implausibly as real people act). I doubt that many readers will think them real; the husband of the heroine never seems so, and the heroine is first of all a sort of symbiotic state of the poet. (You feel, "Yes, Robert Lowell would act like this if he were a girl"; but whoever saw a girl like Robert Lowell?)

Occasionally, for a few lines, the poem becomes so academic and clumsy that one is astonished: "My husband was a fool/ To run out from the Navy when disgrace/ Still wanted zeal to look him in the face." I do not believe that even Cotton Mather ever managed to think in the style of that last line. If I quote a similar passage—"Soon enough we saw/ Death like the Bourbon after Waterloo,/ Who learning and forgetting nothing, knew/ Nothing but ruin. Why must we mistrust/ Ourselves with Death who takes the world on trust?/ Although God's brother, and himself a god,/ Death whipped his horses through the startled sod;/ For neither conscience nor omniscience warned/ Him from his folly, when the virgin scorned/ His courtship, and the quaking earth revealed/ Death's desperation to the Thracian field"—and then tell the reader that these rather labored and academic lines are three-fourths of the *last stanza* of the poem, I won't blame him for looking unbelieving.

The poem is hurt very much by being a sort of anthology of favorite Lowell effects—situations are repeated, there is even a passage adapted from an earlier poem; the reader gets confused and thinks, "Am I in 'Her Dead Brother' now? Here's the stove, but where's the suicide? Isn't this 'David and Bathsheba' now?" What Mr. Lowell is attempting to do in this poem is often beyond his powers and knowledge (where narrative verse is concerned everybody alive is an amateur, though Frost was a professional thirty years ago); usually the poet is having to try much too hard, so that one does not feel very often in this poem the spontaneity, the live half-accidental half-providential rightness, that some of the best poetry has or seems to have. Sometimes Mr. Lowell is having great difficulties, and sometimes he is seeking refuge from them in some of the effects that he has produced so well and so often before.

He is a poet of both Will and Imagination, but his Will is always seizing his Imagination by the shoulders and saying to it in a grating voice: "Don't sit there fooling around; *get to work!*" —and his poor Imagination gets tense all over and begins to revolve determinedly and familiarly, like a squirrel in a squirrelcage. Goethe talked about the half-somnambulistic state of the poet; but Mr. Lowell too often is either having a nightmare or else is wide awake gritting his teeth and working away at All The Things He Does Best. Cocteau said to poets: *Learn what you can do and then don't do it;* and this is so—we do it enough without trying. As a poet Mr. Lowell sometimes doesn't have enough trust in God and tries to do everything himself: he proposes *and* disposes—and this helps to give a certain monotony to his work. But probably the reader will want to say to me, by now, what Lincoln said about the drunkard Grant: "If I knew his brand I would order my other generals a barrel." And I have put my objections to his long poem rather too strongly; it is a powerful and impressive poem, with a good many beautiful or touching passages and a great many overwhelming ones, one of the better poems of one of the best of living poets.

Paterson (Book I) seemed to me a wonderful poem; I should not have supposed beforehand that William Carlos Williams could do the organizing and criticizing and selecting that a work of this length requires. Of course, Book I is not organized quite so well as a long poem *ought* to be, but this is almost a defining characteristic of long poems—and I do not see how anyone could do better using only those rather mosaic organizational techniques that Dr. Williams employs, and neglecting as much as he does narrative, drama, logic, and sustained movement, the primary organizers of long poems. I waited for the next three books of *Paterson* more or less as you wait for someone who has gone to break the bank at Monte Carlo for the second, third, and fourth times; I was afraid that I knew what was going to happen, but I kept wishing as hard as I could that it wouldn't.

Now that Book IV has been printed, one can come to some conclusions about *Paterson* as a whole. My first conclusion is this: it doesn't seem to *be* a whole; my second: *Paterson* has been getting rather steadily worse. Most of Book IV is much worse than II and III, and neither of them even begins to compare with Book I. Book IV is so disappointing that I do not want to write about it at any length: it would not satisfactorily conclude even a quite mediocre poem. Both form and content often seem a parody of those of the "real" *Paterson;* many sections have a scrappy inconsequence, an arbitrary irrelevance, that is extraordinary; poetry of the quality of that in Book I is almost completely lacking—though the forty lines about a new Odysseus coming in from the sea are particularly good, and there are other fits and starts of excellence. There are in Part III long sections of a measure that sounds exactly like the stuff you produce when you are demonstrating to a class that any prose whatsoever can be converted into four-stress accentual verse simply by inserting line-endings every four stresses. These sections *look* like blank verse, but are flatter than the flattest blank verse I have ever read—for instance: "Branching trees and ample gardens gave/ the village streets a delightful charm and/ the narrow old-fashioned brick walls added/ a dignity to the shading trees. It was a fair/ resort for summer sojourners on their way/ to the Falls, the main object of interest." This passage suggests that the guidebook of today is the epic of tomorrow; and a worse possibility, the telephone book put into accentual verse, weighs upon one's spirit.

Books II and III are much better than this, of course: Book II is decidedly what people call "a solid piece of work," but most of the magic is gone. And one begins to be very doubtful about the organization: should there be so much of the evangelist and his sermon? Sould so much of this book consist of what are—the reader is forced to conclude—real letters from a real woman? One reads these letters with involved, embarrassed pity, quite as if she had walked into the room and handed them to one. What has been done to them to make it possible for us to respond to them as art, not as raw reality? to make them part of the poem *Paterson*? I can think of no answer except: "They have been copied out on the typewriter." Anyone can object, "But the context makes them part of the poem"; and anyone can reply to this objection, "It takes a lot of context to make somebody else's eight-page letter the conclusion to a book of a poem."

Book II introduces—how one's heart sinks!—Credit and Usury, those enemies of man, God, and contemporary long poems. Dr. Williams has always put up a sturdy resistance to Pound when Pound has recommended to him Santa Sophia or the Parthenon, rhyme or metre, European things like that; yet he takes Credit and Usury over from Pound and gives them a good home and maintains them in practically the style to which they have been accustomed—his motto seems to be, *I'll adopt your child if only he's ugly enough*. It is interesting to see how much some later parts of *Paterson* resemble in their structure some middle and later parts of the *Cantos:* the Organization of Irrelevance (or, perhaps, the Irrelevance of Organization) suggests itself as a name for this category of structure. Such organization is *ex post facto* organization: if something is somewhere, one can always find Some Good Reason for its being there, but if it had not been there would one reader have missed it? if it had been put somewhere else, would one reader have guessed where it should have "really" gone? Sometimes these anecdotes, political remarks, random comments seem to be where they are for one reason: because Dr. Williams chose—happened to choose— for them to be there. One is reminded of that other world in which Milton found Chance "sole arbiter."

Book III is helped very much by the inclusion of "Beautiful Thing," that long, extremely effective lyric that was always intended for *Paterson;* and Book III, though neither so homogeneous nor so close to Book I, is in some respects superior to Book II. But all three later books are worse organized, more eccentric and idiosyncratic, more self-indulgent, than the first. And yet that is not the point, the real point: the *poetry*, the lyric rightness, the queer wit, the improbable and dazzling perfection of so much of Book I have disappeared—or at least, reappear only fitfully. Early in Book IV, while talking to his son, Dr. Williams quotes this to him: "What I miss, said your mother, is the poetry, the pure poem of the first parts." She is right.

I have written a good deal about Dr. Williams' unusual virtues, so I will take it for granted that I don't need to try to demonstrate, all over again, that he is one of the best poets alive. He was the last of the good poets of his generation to become properly appreciated; and some of his appreciators, in the blush of conversion, rather overvalue him now. When one reads that no "living American poet has written anything better and more ambitious" than *Paterson*, and that Dr. Williams is a poet who gives us "just about everything," one feels that the writer has in some sense missed the whole point of William Carlos Williams. He is a *very* good but *very* limited poet, particularly in vertical range. He is a notably unreasoning, intuitive writer—is not, of course, an intellectual in any sense of the word; and he has further limited himself by volunteering for and organizing a long dreary imaginary war in which America and the Present are fighting against Europe and the Past. But go a few hundred years back inside the most American American and it is Europe: Dr. Williams is just as much Darkest Europe as any of us, down there in the middle of his past.

In his long one-sided war with Eliot Dr. Williams seems to me to come off badly—particularly so when we compare the whole of *Paterson* with the *Four Quartets*. When we read the *Four Quartets* we are reading the long poem of a poet so temperamentally isolated that he does not even put another character, another human being treated at length, into the whole poem;

and yet the poem (probably the best long poem since the *Duino Elegies*) impresses us not with its limitations but with its range and elevation, with how much it knows not simply about men but about Man—not simply about one city or one country but about the West, that West of which America is no more than the last part.

The Situation of a Poet

NOWADAYS most readers of poetry think Dr. Williams one
of the best and most original of American poets, so the
critic no longer needs to say that these collected poems *are*
poems, and sometimes wonderful ones, but can talk quietly and
inconclusively about their strengths and weaknesses and
strangenesses, the unusual qualities that make them what they
are. For this poet is as odd as he is good; when you compare him
with the writers whom at his best he deserves to be compared
with, the good poets of other times and places, he is in some ways
surprisingly different.

He is, just as many of them were, as magically observant and
mimetic as a good novelist, though his range of observation is
different. He reproduces the details of what he sees with surprising freshness, clarity, and economy; and he sees as extraordinarily, sometimes, the *Gestalten* of this earth, the spirit
moving behind the letters. In spite of writing almost exclusively
in "free verse"—which seems to mean, mostly, accentual verse,

not very often regular—he is one of the most tensile, dynamic, and kinesthetically engaging of poets; his quick transparent lines have a nervous and contracted strength. Often they move as jerkily and intently as a bird, though they can sleep as calmly as a bird, too; they do not have the flowing and easy strength, the rhythmic powers in reserve, the envelopment and embodiment, of some of the verse of older poets. But sometimes they have a marvellous delicacy and gentleness, a tact of pure showing; how well he calls into existence our precarious, confused, partial looking out at the world—our being-here-looking, just looking! And if he is often pure presentation, he is often pure exclamation, and delights in yanking something into life with a galvanic imperative or interjection. This is reflected in his reading: he reads poems successfully but unconventionally, without indicating most line-endings, and sounds like an urgent but delicately graduated riveting-machine. All this proceeds from the whole bent of his nature: he prefers a clear, active, intense confusion to any "wise passiveness," to any calm and clouded two-sidedness—whenever he sees that there is something to be said for both sides, he speaks up for the underdog, hard, so that his work is a Permanent Revolution of an anarchist emotional kind, and he himself spins willingly on the wheel of things.

He loves to tell the disgraceful or absurd or obscene or piercing or exhilarating or animally delightful truth. He is neither wise nor intellectual, but is full of homely shrewdness and common sense, of sharply intelligent comments dancing cheek-to-cheek with prejudice and random eccentricity; he is somebody who, sometimes, does see what things are like, and he is able to say what he sees more often than most poets, since his methods permit (indeed encourage) him to say anything at all without worrying: *Can* one say such things in poetry? in this particular poem? Any selection of his best fifteen or twenty poems would be notably unjust to him, since so many of his best perceptions exist in slight or fragmentary form—vignettes are things we associate with perished essayists, but there has never been an Occidental poet who specialized more in them, or was much better at them. We pause, rather than remain, in most of his poems: they do not give us a big, secure, formed, regularly rhythmed world to rest in, and we fall from one homogeneity of instant occasion into another. In the old poems that we value most there is a formal and meaningful relationship between the whole and parts that is often missing (though occasionally merely harder to perceive) in Dr. Williams' poems. Often it is arbitrariness, chanciness, mere contingency, that is most directly noticeable in his poems, since this is what impresses us most immediately about the world—and, consequently, about literature that closely copies the world. But the humor and sadness and raw absurdity of things, and the things themselves, exist in startling reality in his best poems.

He has an extraordinary way with, gift for, language. All sizes of contrasts, of grotesque and incongruous relationships, of the rhetoric of both words and things, are there to bring his speech into life; and he has learned—partly from Pound, I imagine—to use Latin abstractions or generalizations with firm and sensuous ease. But his powers are as intermittent as they are extraordinary; he can begin a poem, "The link between Barnum and Calas/ is the freak/ against which Rexroth rages,/

the six-headed cow, the legless woman,/ for each presents a
social concept/ Seeking approval, a pioneer society/ and a
modern asserting the norm/ by stress of the Minotaur." I get
from this diary-prose or reference shorthand only one thing, the
phrase *the link between Barnum and Calas*, which is a witty and
unjust description of Dr. Williams himself, the Oldest Inhabit-
ant of (and only general practitioner along) the Middle Atlantic
sea-coast of Bohemia.

The situation he writes about most is the situation of the poet
—that is, the situation of one particular poet in one particular
country. His world is his own city, with its plants and animals
in yards and vacant lots and outlying fields, its children and
grown-ups in streets and factories and bedrooms—and with the
poet there, there everywhere, sensuous and nervously responsive
and impatiently active, at once their image and their opposite,
full of anger and dismay and absolute acceptance. America is his
own family, so that he says awful things about it but cannot bear
for anyone else to; and he is always saying, too, that it is better
than everything, is everything. But he is ill at ease in Zion, both
in our republic and in the republic of letters; he looks at the poets
along his street in time more distrustfully, though, than he
looks at the people along his street in Paterson. He is as American as even he himself could wish, and cannot resist constantly
bringing up (in the poems themselves, often) the "problem" of
how modern American poets should write poetry, and answering that they must *be* modern and *be* American. He might
as well wish for the nineteenth century to be over: no one but an
antiquarian longing for the experimentalism of the days of the
first World War would complain that American poetry isn't

modern enough; and our poetry has been so American, for so long now, that English critics and readers regard it almost as a foreign poetry in a foreign language, and regret its influence on their own. Dr. Williams often demands the creation of a new language that American poets can write in, one that will really express America. But he is already writing in it, and so are they; all of them speak (to borrow a phrase from a dead Englishman) "choice American," a later and livelier sister of English.

He shows you to yourself as "a creature unlike the others, something/ extraordinary in its vulgarity,/ something strange, unnatural to/ the world, that suffers the world poorly,/ is tripped at home, disciplined at/ the office, greedily eats money —/ for a purpose: to escape the tyranny/ of lies." He speaks for the Resistance or Underground inside each of us, for the ordinary man made immediately and hurtingly and defensively conscious of himself, for the raw animal suddenly become a human being, a citizen, and a poet. Yet things are, perhaps, worse than he says: is the end of this quotation as true as the rest of it? And things are, surely, better than he says: isn't our intermittent lack of vulgarity even more extraordinary than our vulgarity? He says in another poem, approvingly: "The revolution has been accomplished: *noble*/ has been changed to *no bull*." The forbearance of any valuable existence, all that we do not do and do not say for—as Whitman would say—"for reasons," do not have justice done to them by Dr. Williams, who conserves little, and who distrusts any part of the past that he has not made his own particular possession; he keeps too much to that tenth of the iceberg that is above water, perhaps. In the same way, he is a great inventor and refiner and perfecter of poetic techniques, but dismisses as "stale" the great body of poetic techniques that dead poets, from Homer to Rilke, have invented and refined and perfected. So far as organization and metre and rhyme are concerned, he is a sort of homeopath or chiropractor impatient of anything but his own fragment of the truth. Yet it is such a wonderful and individual fragment, an eighth- or quarter-truth so magnificently suited to a special case, that we cannot help feeling that his illusion about form is one of those "necessary heuristic fictions" of the scientist. If you have gone to the moon in a Fourth of July rocket you built yourself, you can be forgiven for looking askance at Pegasus.

In the best of these poems and in the first and best parts of *Paterson*, Dr. Williams is one of the clearest and firmest and queerest, the most human and real, of the poets of our time. If you want to know how the Muse, "install'd here amid the kitchenware" of a New World, already half recovered from the nausea of departure, already swearing soberly (in a voice with hardly a trace of accent) that she will uphold the laws of this republic—if you want to know how the Muse sounds in such a situation, here is one good place to find out.